HAPPY VALLEY
OREGON

HAPPY VALLEY
OREGON
· A BRIEF HISTORY ·

MARK W. HURLBURT

THE
History
PRESS

Published by The History Press
Charleston, SC
www.historypress.com

Copyright © 2023 by Mark W. Hurlburt
All rights reserved

First published 2023

Manufactured in the United States

ISBN 9781467154901

Library of Congress Control Number: 2023937166

To Mom and Dad

CONTENTS

CONTENTS

ACKNOWLEDGEMENTS

I would like to thank the late Karin Morey, my "Jedi Master," for mentoring me in museum work and in local history. The images in this book appear courtesy of the Clackamas County Historical Society, the Wilmer Gardner Research Library, Bud Unruh, Verna Ashton, Mary Ott Piper, Mike Beutler, Erik Gustafsson, the City of Happy Valley, Jim Hill of the Cascade Pacific Council and the Happy Valley History Collection. A big thank-you to Judy Chambers and Adrian Wegner for their help in contributing to this book. Thank you to everyone who has shared their stories and photos with me over the years in compiling and preserving the history of Happy Valley. Thank you to Steve Campbell at the City of Happy Valley for being my contact at city hall for many years and helping me whenever I needed help in researching or exhibiting the history of the city. Thank you to Marilyn Smelser for providing me with priceless materials essential to preserving the history of the city. Thank you to everyone for reading this book, and enjoy the history!

INTRODUCTION

D o you know about a place called Happy Valley, Oregon? Yeah, it's in Harney County. Wait, what? Yes, there was a time when if you heard someone talk about "Happy Valley," it likely was not the one in northern Clackamas County but rather a remote valley in the southeastern part of the state. In 1966, the *Oregonian* described the little city on Portland's doorstep: "Although just outside the boundaries of metro Portland, this Happy Valley is even less known than the other one way over in the Harney County desert country."[1] At that time, Happy Valley's identity was that of an isolated, rural, widely unknown farming community. It stayed that way until the 1990s, when it began to transform into an urban, rapidly developing city of residences and commercial growth. If you are someone who thought Happy Valley began in the 1990s and it didn't even exist before then, I can understand why. The city seemed to emerge out of nowhere and quickly became one of the most popular places to live in and move to in early twenty-first-century Oregon. Happy Valley incorporated as a municipality in 1965 and began as a pioneer settlement in 1851. Some of you may be shocked by that. But it's true.

I am a lifelong Happy Valley resident, thanks to my father. He purchased property in Happy Valley in 1970. It was a vacant lot with views of open land and not many other houses. The place was set in the shadow of Scouters Mountain on part of Christian and Matilda Deardorff's old donation land claim, the first American pioneers to settle in Happy Valley. My father then had his house built, planted every tree and bush on his parcel of land and raised his family. He found the perfect place to call home. Because we never moved, all of my experiences growing up were in the same house, with the same back and front yards and the same city. I grew up cultivating a sentimental feeling not only for the home my father established but also for the community that surrounded it. I spent my childhood personally witnessing the land once occupied by barns, horses and pastures get bulldozed into subdivisions. The small residential city expanded and grew to welcome businesses and change. As the way Happy Valley once was quickly faded into the past, my future would become one interested in remembering the events that shaped me and asking questions and making discoveries about the people who came before I was around.

My enjoyment for learning history sprouted during my freshman year at Clackamas High School. I was part of the first student class to spend their entire four-year career at the new high school building built along 122nd Avenue in Clackamas. My favorite subject was—you guessed it— history, thanks to my teacher Mrs. McFarlane. Her history class was fun and interesting and strengthened my curiosity. She made me realize that history isn't just about memorizing names and dates; it's a collection of real-life stories passed from one generation to the next to understand who we are and how a place became what it is. Thanks to this inspiration, I studied and earned a bachelor's degree in history from Portland State University. While in school, I mostly learned about United States and world history. But what I found myself most interested in was local history. I was learning about what happened far away on the other side of the country and the world, but I wondered—did anything happen around here? I didn't really realize that Happy Valley had much of a history to tell until after I started working for the Clackamas County Historical Society at the Museum of the Oregon Territory in Oregon City. In the research library I discovered on one of the shelves, to my amazement, a book called *The History of Happy Valley, Oregon: 1851–1969*. It was a project completed by the Happy Valley Grade School students in 1969. This book inspired me even more to research, collect, exhibit and write about my hometown's history.

Among the items I collected over the years were photographs of the area. Some of these were taken by a longtime Happy Valley resident named Bud Unruh, who captured what the city and area looked like in the late 1980s and early 1990s, prior to the city's pro-growth development. In 2014, I asked Mr. Unruh if he could return to some of those same spots he took photos of many years earlier and capture new ones for a before-and-after comparison. He did just that and presented his photos to me for my collection. Over the years, I continued to collect photos, artifacts and stories and interview people with knowledge of Happy Valley's past. I started writing articles that were published by the *Clackamas Review* and the City of Happy Valley and eventually reached the point where I could have enough for a book. This work is a culmination of twelve years of research that began when I started at the Clackamas County Historical Society in 2011.

Keep in mind, this book is written from my unique perspective, different from the perspective of the grade school students who compiled the history of Happy Valley for their book in 1969 and different from someone else several years older than me. I'm not an expert. I'm just someone who enjoys exploring history and learning more about the area I call home. For those who think history is boring or don't know what it is, history can be something as simple as telling a story. Here's an example. During my kindergarten year at Happy Valley Elementary School, I fell asleep riding home on the school bus. This was the first time I rode the bus home by myself, as my sister had gone hunting with our dad. The bus stopped at my house and my mom waited for me, but the bus drove away without me getting off. She was obviously confused and concerned. The bus returned to the school, where the driver discovered me asleep and woke me up. I was turned over to the principal, Mr. Orme, who was still at the school. My mom drove there to find out what happened and was relieved when she found me safe. This is an experience I still remember, and it tells a good story with a lesson to be learned. This is what I've learned: history happens every day. History is remembering. We remember our stories. Our stories emerge from our experiences. Our experiences teach us lessons about ourselves and each other. Every person and place has a story. This is a story of Happy Valley, Oregon.

Chapter 1

VOLCANIC AND WILD

A Natural History

To understand how Happy Valley came to be what it is today, we must go back to its volcanic formation. The Boring Volcanic Field, named after the community of Boring in Clackamas County, consists of volcanic sites across the Portland metro area and began erupting about three million years ago. The sites of volcanic eruptions, known as vents, caused basaltic flows that formed small conical shapes constructed of volcanic cinders, known as cinder cones. Thousands of years prior to the first human inhabitants to live in the area that would become the City of Happy Valley, lava eruptions and flows in the Boring Volcanic Field formed the hills that stand out today as regional landmarks. One of these cinder cones, known as Mount Scott, rises more than 1,000 feet above sea level.[2] Mount Talbert, which can be seen overlooking vehicles driving along Sunnyside Road, is a cinder cone that reaches an elevation of 740 feet. Scott and Talbert are also buttes, which are isolated hills with steep vertical sides and relatively flat tops. Nearby, a knoll known as Scouters Mountain reaches about 700 feet above sea level. It is an extinct lava dome that formed with mounded lava over a vent without flowing. The formations of Mount Scott and Scouters Mountain and the ridges between them formed the shape of a bowl, also referred to as a hollow or valley, with fertile soil and several springs of water that would attract wildlife and humans.

The Happy Valley area features several natural sources of life-giving water. A stream that originates from springs in the valley bowl received the name Mount Scott Creek. From the Happy Valley wetland, this creek

Overlooking the valley bowl from Mount Scott toward Scouters Mountain in 1992. *Bud Unruh.*

flows through a grove of western red cedar trees southward by Mount Talbert until its confluence with Kellogg Creek just south of the city of Milwaukie.[3] Multiple springs emerging from Scouters Mountain would later provide water for several farmers and for children attending the first school in Happy Valley. To the east of the valley bowl, another source of water called Rock Creek flows southwesterly. Along its route, the creek naturally plunges over a twenty-two-foot waterfall and continues about one mile until its confluence with the Clackamas River. Downstream of the waterfall, several fish species such as steelhead, Coho salmon, trout, pacific lamprey and northern pike minnow have been noted to use the creek for habitat.[4] To help offset disruptions and damage caused by human interference to fish habitat, groups such as Clackamas County Water Environment Services, Clackamas River Basin Council, Stop Oregon Litter and Vandalism (SOLVE), Oregon Department of Fish and Wildlife (ODFW) and the City of Happy Valley have all worked to protect the fish habitat in Rock Creek near its confluence with the Clackamas River. Their work has included placing numerous large wood structures and boulders at the creek to provide protective cover and create deep pools for young salmon to grow before journeying to the Pacific Ocean.[5]

The fertile soil of the Happy Valley area also sprouted numerous types of varying vegetation. The valley bowl was once covered with timber. As part of their history of Happy Valley project in 1969, the Happy Valley Grade School students recorded these trees as including Douglas firs, pines, spruces, cedars, alders, oaks and maples. Some of the wildflowers that were once abundant in the valley included trilliums, violets, wild iris, lady slippers, buttercups, daisies, bachelor's buttons and dandelions. A plentiful amount of wild berries also populated Mount Scott, Scouters Mountain and the valley between them. These included strawberries, blackberries, raspberries and huckleberries. Hazelnuts and black walnuts were also noted as being available for consumption by any interested animal or human.[6] The rest of the valley area was occupied by tall grass, shrubs and bushes.

Altogether, Happy Valley's terrain has served as an excellent home for several wildlife species to live and thrive. Some of the mammals recorded as having lived in the area include deer, beavers, raccoons, badgers, minks, rabbits, squirrels, opossums, muskrats, weasels, foxes, coyotes and bobcats. Black bears also once lived in the area, as Happy Valley featured the ideal habitat and food sources to feed their omnivorous diet of nuts, fruit, berries, bugs, fish and more. Skunks, unmistakable by their tuxedo color and odor, apparently were for a time commonly seen in the area. Should one ever cross your path, wisely retreat in the opposite direction before its musk is unleashed. Although rare, mountain lions have been reported prowling in and around the area since the days of the pioneer settlers. The territorial hunters usually try to avoid human interactions, but sightings in the city have occurred as recently as 2014 near Ridgecrest Road and in 2022 outside a residence.[7]

Birds of many varieties have been sighted in Happy Valley since the earliest pioneers and into the twenty-first century. The settlers are known to have hunted gamebirds such as pheasants, grouse, quail and turkeys. Birds of prey such as bald eagles, red-tailed hawks and great horned owls were once commonly seen or heard at night. Some of the other types of birds that have been recorded or known to have called Happy Valley home include western meadowlarks, wrens, sparrows, black-capped chickadees, American robins, Steller's Jays, bob-o-links, mallard ducks, red-winged blackbirds and hummingbirds.[8]

Some of the wildlife that have lived in the Happy Valley area after the turn of the twenty-first century include the does and bucks of rabbits, which are excellent at multiplying; squirrels, which are commonly seen scurrying across roads and in parks always in search of nuts; nutria, large rodents with the look of a beaver with rat-like tails that can be found at ponds and streams; mallard ducks, which always quack up visitors to the pond at the Happy Valley Park wetland; and garter snakes, which are harmless, but that matters not to those suffering from ophidiophobia, or fear of snakes. Raccoons, who usually live in hollowed trees, are excellent climbers, runners and swimmers. This nocturnal omnivorous mammal prowls along wooded

Ducks greeting a visitor to the pond at the Happy Valley Park wetland. *Happy Valley History Collection.*

streams, in wetlands and in people's yards in search for any food it can grab with its adept fingers. Opossums, a marsupial, can be seen at night feeding on insects, frogs, snakes, small mammals and fruits. Deer, usually the white-tailed species, can still be viewed on increasingly rare occasions in wooded areas and enjoying people's gardens and fruit trees. Bats can be seen at dusk catching mosquitos and other insects. A majestic hawk can be seen soaring over the valley every once in a while, scoping for small critters. The hoot of an owl can also be heard after dark coming from Scouters Mountain and Mount Talbert Nature Parks. The yips and howls from clever coyotes are still heard echoing from the Happy Valley Park wetland during the night, when they might be on the hunt for rabbits, mice, squirrels and other small animals, including deer fawns. Although some of the wild flora and fauna that once thrived in Happy Valley remain, it's not as it once was as the area became a place for human residence.

Chapter 2

THE DEARDORFFS AND THE FIRST PEOPLE IN HAPPY VALLEY

P rior to the establishment of an American pioneer settlement, the Indigenous inhabitants of the area that would become known as Happy Valley were the Clackamas people of the Chinookan-speaking language group. These Native Americans lived on the land stretching from the Willamette River to the Cascade foothills and from the Columbia River south to Willamette Falls.[9] The Clackamas were among the Indigenous people who fished at the falls from platforms using nets and spears to catch salmon leaping over the falls.[10] In the Chinook language, the *Clackamas* name referred to the people who lived in the Clackamas River region.[11] This river flows about a mile south of Sunnyside Road at its closest point. Early European and American explorers estimated the population of the Clackamas to be about two thousand people. By 1855, only eighty-eight of the Clackamas people remained. Their population plummeted due to a lack of immunity to diseases introduced by British and American explorers and settlers. An 1855 treaty by Willamette Valley tribes, including the Clackamas, ceded the land to the United States government, and they were soon forcibly relocated to the Grand Ronde Reservation in western Oregon.[12]

Some of the artifacts the Indigenous people left behind included arrow points found at the dam on the property of Wally Hubbard just off 142nd Avenue south of Sunnyside Road and in a cave on Mount Talbert. David Hanset and his son Allen in the Sunnyside area of Clackamas, found Indian arrow points, flint and obsidian in their backyard. Local farmers also gave the Hanset family Indigenous artifacts found while plowing their fields. David

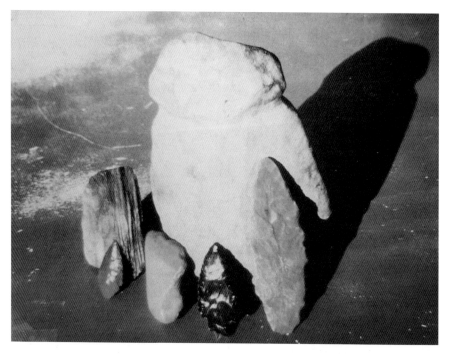

Arrow points and relics found at Wally Hubbard's dam near 142nd Avenue south of Sunnyside Road. *Verna Ashton.*

recalled hearing stories of the Boy Scouts exploring the Mount Talbert cave several years earlier. His son Allen hiked across Mount Talbert in search of the cave in the late 1970s. Allen found the cave by a cliff on the southwest side of the butte. The entrance was only two and a half feet tall and was covered with vegetation. The cave's ceiling was five feet tall and the interior about twenty-two feet long and fourteen feet wide. Allen found a redstone arrow point and a bear's tooth inside with a vent hole in a corner of the cave that could have served as a chimney.[13]

The homeland the Clackamas people were forced to leave proceeded to transform into American pioneer settlements, one of which formed in Happy Valley. In 1850, the Donation Land Claim Act was passed by the United States Congress as a way of encouraging Americans to migrate to the new U.S. Territory of Oregon, which was established in 1848. The act granted to settlers or occupants of public lands—who were white or half American Indian, at least eighteen years of age and United States citizens—320 acres to an individual and 640 acres to a married couple for those living in Oregon prior to December 1, 1850, to legitimize the claims offered by Oregon's provisional government. After that date and prior to the act's expiration in 1855, the land offered was halved to 160 acres for an individual and 320 acres for a married couple. The Deardorff family would use the act to claim hundreds of acres and be the first to settle in what would eventually become Happy Valley.

Christian Deardorff, of German ancestry, was born in Virginia on January 15, 1805. He was the first of thirteen children born to John and Catharine Deardorff. His future wife, Matilda Landers, was born in Virginia on August 31, 1802, to Christian and Elizabeth Landers. Christian and Matilda Deardorff married in January 1824 in Indiana, where they had the first of their children, John Martindale, who was born in October of that year. The Deardorffs' other children included David, Tobias, James and Rebecca. While in Indiana, Christian worked as a farmer and a miller.[14] The family also lived in Illinois before going overland from Iowa to the Oregon Territory in a train of thirty wagons. The Deardorffs arrived in Oregon in October 1850.[15]

In 1851, Christian and Matilda Deardorff settled on 640 acres in Clackamas County in the valley tucked between Mount Scott and Scouters Mountain. Available land from the Donation Land Claim Act and springs of water were the reasons why the Deardorffs settled in the valley bowl.[16] As they were the first American pioneers to settle there, the area became known as the Deardorff Valley, Deardorff Settlement and Christilla Valley, a combination of Christian (Chris) and Matilda (Tilla). Christian then continued his trade as a farmer. As other pioneers joined the Deardorffs and settled in and near the valley, the area became a farming community. In October 1851, John M. Deardorff claimed 320 acres in the valley bordering his parents' claim. After he settled in the valley, John M. walked to Milwaukie to work in splitting rails. John M. officially settled his claim at the land office in Oregon City in December 1851, followed by Christian in January 1852.[17]

In 1852, a man whose identity is unknown and who traveled the Oregon Trail with the Deardorffs in the same wagon train passed away and needed to be laid to rest somewhere. He lived nearby and had no family. John M. Deardorff donated a small part on the eastern side of his land claim for the man to be buried, and the site became a cemetery.[18] A marker that said, "Covered Wagon Pioneer 1852" was placed on his gravesite. Located on Scouters Mountain, the cemetery become known as the Christilla Pioneer Cemetery and was later renamed the Deardorff Pioneer Cemetery. This is where Christian (died in 1884), Matilda (died in 1891) and other Deardorff family members would be buried. Because of vandals damaging and

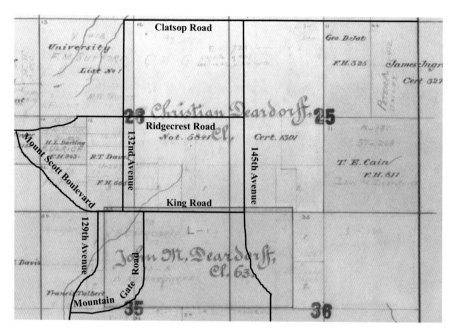

A map showing the donation land claims of Christian and John M. Deardorff overlaid with present-day road locations. *Clackamas County Historical Society.*

removing some of the markers in the mid-twentieth century, two Deardorff descendants, Mabel Cockle and Annette Deardorff, formed the Christilla Pioneer Cemetery Association to help restore the cemetery.[19] The family recorded the gravesite locations and asked the Boy Scouts, who had a camp nearby, to take care of the cemetery. Although five acres were donated to be used for the cemetery, only a small part was actually used for the graves, which became protected by a fence beginning in the 1960s.[20] Deardorff descendant Edith Guidi was the last burial in the cemetery, in 1932, until Amanda Wright, an infant who passed in 1988, was buried there. The cemetery is located peacefully surrounded by a natural wooded area, a tranquil memorial of the settlement founded by the Deardorff family.

In 1854, John M. Deardorff married Rachel Ingram, a native of Illinois and daughter of James Ingram who journeyed the Oregon Trail in 1852 and settled on a donation land claim to the northeast of the Christian Deardorff claim.[21] John M. and Rachel Deardorff had sons John Bennett, William Albert and James Henry and a daughter, Matilda, who died in infancy. John and Rachel were usually not referred to as Mr. and Mrs. Deardorff. They were more often called "Uncle John and Aunt Rachel" in the community. In 1858, the family built the famous Deardorff barn on John's dairy farm,

John M. Deardorff. *Happy Valley History Collection.*

which stood until 1997, when it was torn down to make way for the Happy Valley Heights subdivision.[22] The barn was built in a Vernacular style with hewn and mortised timbers fastened together with pegs and the siding attached using square nails. John M. also built a little milk house over the spring on his claim to store milk jars and butter in the cold water to prevent them from spoiling.[23] There was also a large dryer house used for drying fruit, an apple house for storing apples and a mill to grind them into cider. The big barn was used for storing bags of potatoes and bins of oats and wheat.[24]

As part of his occupation as a farmer, John M. Deardorff would make a weekly trip into Portland with his horse and buggy to sell produce from the farm.[25] Like his father, William Albert made regular deliveries of produce to Portland by horse and buggy. But with only a steep, muddy road over Mount Scott as the way out of the valley, William and another local resident, C.W. Gay, petitioned county commissioners in 1898 to have a new county road surveyed and constructed going north to Foster Road. John Bennett worked as one of the axe men in the survey and laying of the road that was a joint effort by both Multnomah and Clackamas Counties.[26] The road on the Clackamas side would become known as 132nd Avenue and on the Multnomah side would become known as Deardorff Road.

For school, children of the valley first went to Sunnyside and Rock Creek. But in 1892, a small one-room schoolhouse opened on one acre of land donated to the county from John M. Deardorff's land claim.[27] John Bennett Deardorff, who was the school district's clerk, got a large bell made to be placed in the steeple.[28] This bell continued on when the schoolhouse was replaced by a larger one in 1917 on the same site, which was added on to over the decades to keep pace with the valley's population.[29] When the new Happy Valley Elementary School was built in 2008, the Deardorff bell remained on display outside the school on the same land as the original schoolhouse.

Rachel Deardorff passed away in 1901. By this time, her sons James and William Albert had moved away to Santa Ana, California, and her husband, John, had turned control over the family farm to their son John Bennett,

The Deardorff barn as it appeared in 1989 prior to its demolition to make way for the Happy Valley Heights subdivision. *Bud Unruh.*

who still lived there.[30] John M. Deardorff, cofounder of the settlement that would become the City of Happy Valley, died in 1902 and was buried in the cemetery on Scouters Mountain. While members of the first family to set up donation land claims in the hollow passed away, they left a legacy of having created a community of farmers that would eventually become the City of Happy Valley.

Chapter 3

A VALLEY OF FARMERS

Like the Deardorffs, when American pioneer settlers reached the land that would become Happy Valley, they commenced the profession of farming. The availability of springs and fertile soil made it an ideal location for anyone looking to establish a farm. As an increasing number of settlers moved into the valley and claimed acreage, a settlement of farmers formed and became a peaceful community of neighbors.

In 1912, resident Herman Kanne described the valley of farmers he lived in, which he referred to as "East Mount Scott," one of the early names for Happy Valley. He wrote:

> *The district comprises about two square miles, lying partly in the valley and partly on the slope of the hills, by which it is surrounded on all sides. The soil is of a black nature, very loose, without gravel or rock, the hardpan being about four feet down. It is very easy to work with and cleared and very productive. The land is valued at from $250 to $400 per acre, which is cheaper than any other place a like distance from Portland. The farms at one time being heavy timber and brush but were cleared and built up mostly by their present owners, who are a lot of honest, hard-working people, peaceful and law-abiding.*[31]

Before farms could be established, the settlers first had to clear away the timber and brush that occupied much of the valley floor. The pioneer farmers relied on axes and crosscut saws for felling trees. Another method they used was cutting a ring around a timber base and setting it on fire. The flames would burn through the trunk, and the towering flora would collapse. To clear the valley of stumps, farmers dug around and set them on fire; some even used charges of dynamite to blast them out of the ground.[32] After the land was cleared, the soil was plowed with either an ox or a horse.[33] Acre by acre, the space between Mount Scott and Scouters Mountain transformed from a work of nature into fields and pastures ready for growing crops and raising livestock.

Among the families to move to the area when it was just a valley of farmers included the Talberts. Francis and Amanda Talbert and their family settled along what is now 129th Avenue near Mount Scott Creek in 1852. They would later relocate to Clackamas. In 1888, Frank Strickrott brought his family to the valley because the land was selling at a cheap price. Getting a good deal, the Strickrott family built a log cabin. Frank was born in Germany and later came to the United States in 1860.[34] In 1893, Strickrott had a house built along Mount Scott Boulevard for his wife, Eliza, and their children. By 1983, the house no longer belonged to the Strickrotts. With it being in poor condition, the owner at the time planned on selling the house to the Happy Valley Fire Station so they could set it ablaze and use it for firefighting practice. But the Strickrott family bought the house back, cleaned it up and occupied it again.[35]

A horse team at work on the Strickrott family farm looking east with Scouters Mountain in the background. *Clackamas County Historical Society.*

The John M. Deardorff claim eventually became owned by the Meng family, who operated it as a dairy farm. Christian and Dorothea Meng were both from Switzerland before coming to Oregon.[36] The Meng family used the historic Deardorff barn as a milking shed and for storing hay. Florian Meng (1902–1958), Christian and Dorothea's son, drove a Ford pickup to deliver 140 gallons of milk a day from the farm to a marketing cooperative.[37] Florian married Helen Bower in 1928, and they had sons Donald and Darrell.[38] The Meng brothers reminisced on childhood memories of their old family farm when the Deardorff barn was dismantled in 1997.

Part of the Christian Deardorff land claim would be farmed by Deardorff descendants. One of these descendants was Edith Guidi. Edith was born in 1887 to John Bennett Deardorff, Christian's grandson. Her husband, Abraham "Abe" Guidi, was originally from Italy and came to the United States in about 1899.[39] Their farm was located along 145th Avenue near King Road. Another Deardorff descendant who farmed part of Christian's land claim was Mabel Cockle, also a daughter of John Bennett Deardorff and Edith's younger sister. Mabel and her husband Roy's farm was also along 145th Avenue. Not far away, Andrew Callahan, born in 1859 in Iowa, and his family had a dairy farm on the southern side of what is now Ridgecrest Road from Happy Valley Park to 145th Avenue. The Herman Kanne farm was on the western side of 145th Avenue and later became a boarding facility for horses owned by the Clifford Friesen family. The Guidi, Cockle, Callahan and Kanne farms all shared water from a spring on the lower western slope of Scouters Mountain, which today flows into a water runoff pond in the Happy Valley Park wetland.[40]

A prominent family in Happy Valley was the Zinser family. The Zinsers were from Germany, like several others in the Happy Valley area, and came to the United States in about 1867 to Illinois. In 1890, John George Zinser bought land in Happy Valley and built a house on the spot where the Happy Valley Policing Center is on King Road.[41] This house is where another early family, the Rebstocks, would reside. Karl Charles Rebstock purchased the place in 1901, and it later became known as the Rebstock house. After John George Zinser sold his house to Rebstock, he moved to California and farmed there. George's brother John Chris built a house west of 129th Avenue and south of Mount Scott Boulevard. Chris worked as a teacher at the Carus School south of Oregon City and later moved to Oregon City when he became the county superintendent of public schools.[42] Their brother Charles Frederick Zinser, or "Fred," built a log cabin at the corner of Mount Scott Boulevard and Ridgecrest Road in 1890. Fred then built a house north of the log cabin but relocated it in 1911 and used it as a granary and shop.[43] The third house was built in 1912, but after it burned to the ground in 1920, a fourth house was built. The northern part of Fred and his son Elmer's farms later became part of the Willamette National Cemetery. Fred married Augusta Kanne from the Kanne farm, and they had three children together: Royal, Elmer and Lydia.[44]

Augusta Kanne was a daughter of August and Wilhelmina (Rosenau) Kanne, who had eleven children together, including Herman. August Kanne was born in 1844 in Germany and came to the United States in 1856 with his family and settled in Minnesota, Augusta's birthplace in 1867.

Charles Frederick "Fred" Zinser. *Happy Valley History Collection.*

The Kanne family came to Happy Valley in about 1888, and their farm would later be described as "unquestionably the finest ranch in this part of Clackamas County."[45] Augusta was an active church member who helped organize the evangelical church at the corner of 129th Avenue and Mount Scott Boulevard. She was regarded as one of the most prominent residents of Happy Valley when she passed away from pneumonia in 1925.[46] Fred and Augusta Zinser's daughter Lydia married Normer Peterson from the Peterson-Paulson farm located on the slope south of King Road. Lydia and Normer bought property and farmed the land at the northwest corner of King Road and 145th Avenue.[47] Lydia was a school janitor and teacher for many years. Elmer Zinser married Hazel Knauss in 1923. The Knauss family were from Minnesota and farmed along 129th Avenue. Bertha Knauss, a sister of Hazel's father, Benjamin Knauss, married Karl Charles Rebstock, and they had a family farm along King Road. In 1920, Royal and Elmer purchased thirty acres west of 132nd Avenue and north of Ridgecrest Road. Elmer bought his brother's share, and Elmer and Hazel made their home there. In 1937, they purchased forty acres on 132nd and Clatsop Road to farm. In the 1930s, Elmer got a threshing machine, used for separating grain and oats, and threshed for people in the Happy Valley area. Elmer also had an incubator in the basement of his house for laying hens. Elmer and Hazel had two kids, Doris and Alton.[48] In his later years, Alton "Al" Zinser shared memories and stories of Happy Valley and provided valuable history of his family who was connected to so many other families who lived in the farming community.

During the nineteenth and the first part of the twentieth centuries, when Happy Valley was just a farming community, entire families were able to completely sustain themselves by working on their farms.[49] The settlers and farmers of the area raised almost all their own food. For meat, people would butcher one of their farm animals, such as a cow, lamb or pig. The hunting of deer and other wild game was also common and important in providing food in the days before grocery stores were commonplace.[50] To prepare for wintertime, residents preserved their food by canning and drying their fruits and vegetables and smoking their meats. Residents also made jams and stored their preserved food in jars in a cellar or pantry. This was the main source of food for farming families during the winter. Chickens supplied farmers with eggs, while cows provided them with milk, cream, butter and cheese.[51] In the evenings, as the sun set, the echoing sound of ringing cowbells could be heard across the valley as cows returned to their barns to be milked.[52]

Many different crops were grown by farmers in Happy Valley. Grain was grown to make bread and hay for feeding cows and horses. John M. Deardorff produced buckwheat grain of such excellent grade that he earned the nickname "Buckwheat Deardorff." To market it, he designed a special stamp marked on his grain sacks—a deer's head followed by the syllable "DORFF."[53] When grains were ready to be harvested, they were cut using a scythe before being tossed onto a hay wagon and hauled to a barn. The engine-powered threshing machine eventually made harvest work much quicker and easier.[54] Commonly produced vegetables included beans, peas, potatoes, corn and cabbage. Plentiful fruit trees produced pears, apples, plums, prunes and cherries. Some of the berries that were cultivated included strawberries, boysenberries, blackberries and raspberries.[55] Eva Ulrich Ott reminisced in a 1997 interview that the summer months were busy for picking berries and that her father, William Ulrich (1886–1944), would take them to market on Yamhill Street in Portland. Out-of-towners would also come to Happy Valley with their families and set up tents just to pick berries.[56] According to Herman Kanne in his 1912 description of the valley, each farm covered fifteen to forty acres, with three to six acres in berries and about the same number of acres in orchards.[57]

Happy Valley farmers sold their produce to markets in Portland. Some went to markets on Foster Road in the Lents neighborhood, Yamhill Street or Powell Boulevard to sell their product for cash or trade for goods they

The farmlands of the Happy Valley bowl in 1915 looking toward Mount Scott. *Clackamas County Historical Society.*

needed. The goods they would trade for included sugar, salt, coffee and clothing. The farmers carried their produce in forty-two-pound crates hauled in horse-drawn wagons.[58] In 1906, the Zinser family picked seven forty-two-pound crates of blackberries and more than four tons of strawberries from their farm.[59]

An entire family would work on their farm. Some of the chores children had to do included helping bring in cows from the pasture, feeding chickens, gathering eggs, bringing in firewood and many other helpful things.[60] Pearl Rebstock, daughter of Charles and Bertha Rebstock, had to wash dishes in the morning before going to school.[61] The men of the family usually tended the crops, barns and livestock. They also supplied meat from hunting or butchering. The women were responsible for cooking and gathering vegetables from the garden. They also made most of the clothing worn by their family from homespun cloth. If a shirt or pant was torn, a wife or mother would sew a patch to repair the clothing.[62]

Herman Kanne ended his 1912 letter by encouraging people to move to the valley. He wrote:

> *Now anyone looking for a nice quiet place to live can find it here. Come and investigate before buying elsewhere. We can show you as fine a place to live as anywhere, a place where nearly everybody is out of debt, where everything is tip-top, and everybody making a comfortable living and then some. Come see and be convinced.*[63]

30

As the twentieth century progressed, the number of people moving to Happy Valley slowly increased. Following World War II, the rise in people migrating to the suburbs instigated the breaking up of large farms, which then averaged thirty to forty acres. Rising inflation and incomes made it no longer profitable for Happy Valley area residents to live off and operate their farms. As a result, farmland was gradually divided and sold to people who wanted to operate hobby farms while working in Portland.[64] As more farmland was sold, Happy Valley transitioned from a valley of farms into a developing residential community.

Chapter 4

THE TALBERTS

A Pioneer Family

When driving on Interstate 205 northbound, as you take the off-ramp to Happy Valley and Sunnyside Road, you will see a forested hill on the right side overlooking the highway. This small "mountain" is officially called Mount Talbert. It is home to a beautiful nature park that opened in 2007. The park is home to four miles of trails and serves as a refuge for wildlife and anyone looking for a quick escape from the busy suburban life of Happy Valley and Clackamas that surrounds it. A mystery surrounds this place, as there is no official origin for the name. So who is Mount Talbert named for?

There is no known record of the butte receiving its name from a proclamation or a document naming it in honor of a distinguished person. It is likely, then, that the name emerged from common usage among people living nearby. Prior to being known by the Talbert name, the butte was known by some in the local community as Mount Latourette. This name comes from the prominent Oregon City family who once owned property on Mount Talbert.[65] Could this be true for the origin of the Talbert name as well? If it is, then the answer as to who the butte was named for can be found in a pioneer family who lived in the Happy Valley area and owned property on the butte. This family included Francis Talbert, a pioneer of 1852, who owned a donation land claim of over three hundred acres just to the north of Mount Talbert. The Talbert property was located where 129th Avenue is today between 122nd Avenue and King Road in Happy

Valley. John Talbert, his son, lived on land to the southwest of the butte. Daniel Talbert, another of Francis's sons, owned a homestead on the western slope of Mount Talbert itself.[66] So who was this family?

Francis Talbert was born in 1804 in Virginia. His future wife, Amanda Newbill, was born in about 1811 also in Virginia.[67] Francis had seven children from his first marriage, while Amanda had four girls from her marriage to her first husband, Jonathan Craghead.[68] Both became widowed, and Francis and Amanda Talbert married in Missouri in 1847. Their first child, John Alexander Talbert, was born in Missouri on September 17, 1848. They also had twin boys, but both died in infancy while the family traveled the Oregon Trail. Amanda Talbert was a slave owner in Missouri and freed her slaves when the family left for Oregon in 1852.[69] The family first spent the winter in Milwaukie before settling on a donation land claim by Mount Scott Creek in the southwestern part of the bowl, arriving after the Deardorffs first settled in Happy Valley in 1851.[70] As they resided in Oregon after December 1, 1850, the Talberts settled on more than three hundred acres of free land from the Donation Land Claim Act. The family cut logs and planed timber to build a house, and Francis and Amanda resided there for about twenty years. Francis and Amanda Talbert then moved to Clackamas, which was known as Marshfield at the time, where they lived the remainder of their lives. When they passed away, Francis in 1881 and Amanda in 1900, their deaths were lamented by the local community, as they were both well beloved.[71]

Amanda Talbert. *Wilmer Gardner Research Library.*

John Talbert, their sole surviving child together, was a farmer who lived in Happy Valley with his parents and, like them, later moved to Clackamas, making his home there for about fifty-six years.[72] He then became a prominent figure in the county, serving in public positions. He was a deputy sheriff of Clackamas County from 1879 to 1882 and a county deputy assessor for two years.[73] In 1901, he was elected as the representative for Clackamas in the state legislature.[74] He was also employed for about thirty years in the fish business, establishing federal

John (*at left*) and Daniel Talbert. *Wilmer Gardner Research Library.*

and state hatcheries on the White Salmon, North Umpqua and McKenzie Rivers.[75] In 1870, John married Emma Davis and had three daughters: Mary, Theodora or "Dora" and Jessie.[76] Davis and her family came to Oregon by traveling in a migrant train of sixty-nine wagons leaving Kansas in 1868. The Davis family spent the winter at Sunnyside before moving to Garfield along the Clackamas River.[77] John Talbert died in 1929 and was highly regarded for being a prominent citizen and one of the most well-known residents of northern Clackamas County. His wife, Emma, passed in 1942.

Daniel Talbert, a son of Francis Talbert and John's older half brother, was the family member who owned a homestead claim on the western slope of Mount Talbert. He was born in Kentucky in 1833 and came to Oregon with his family in 1852. In his obituary, he was described as "a veteran of the

Indian wars in Idaho, in which he gave his country heroic service."[78] Daniel also worked as the director of the Clackamas School District for many years. In 1896, he was elected for a fourth time to the position by the voters of the district. Following his election, Talbert's character was described as it "goes to show that he is a good straightforward, honest man."[79] Daniel married Nathalia "Nettie" Goodridge, and they had two children together, Frank and Bertha. Daniel Talbert died in 1915, and he and his wife, as well as John and Emma and Francis and Amanda, were all laid to rest in the Clackamas Pioneer Cemetery.

Did the name for Mount Talbert come from the family who lived on and around there? The naming of Mount Scott, the butte near Mount Talbert, could contradict this reasoning. A man named Jacob Scott had a donation land claim in Sunnyside in the vicinity of Mount Scott, which might lead some to believe the hill was named after him. However, the mount was named in 1889 after *Oregonian* editor Harvey Scott, who owned hundreds of acres on the butte.[80] There is a notable difference between the two though. While Jacob Scott only lived in the vicinity of Mount Scott, Daniel Talbert actually owned property on Mount Talbert itself, which supports the hill being named for him or his family. On a July 1971 Pittmon map of Oregon City and vicinity, Mount Talbert is identified as "Talbert's Hill." Before being known as Scouters Mountain, that hill was known by some locals as "Guidi's Hill," which was the name of a family who had a farm along the slope. This also supports the naming of Mount Talbert for someone by that name who lived there, which Daniel Talbert did. The Talbert family had a long, prominent presence in the local area and were well beloved by their neighbors in Clackamas. The Talberts lived just to the north and west of the hill, with Daniel Talbert in particular owning a homestead on its western slope. The names Mount Scott and Scouters Mountain emerged from persons who owned property on those places, Harvey Scott and the Boy Scouts, respectively. If the name emerged from common usage among local residents, this would support Mount Talbert being named after Daniel Talbert and his prominent pioneer family.

Chapter 5

THE SUNNYSIDE
OF THE MOUNTAIN

While traveling along Sunnyside Road in Happy Valley, when you reach the intersection with 132nd Avenue, you will see the repurposed buildings of a former country store and mill on one side of the road and a grange hall on the other. This was once the center of the Sunnyside community, a former census-designated place now identified with the City of Happy Valley. In 1997, longtime resident Iva Hubbard Cook recalled that Sunnyside got its name because it was located on "the sunny side of the mountain."[81] She, however, did not mention which mountain. Was it named because it was on the sunny side of Mount Scott? Perhaps Mount Talbert? Or Scouters Mountain? Maybe even Mount Hood? We may never know. The population of this community was 6,791 at the 2000 census. By comparison, the Sunnyside population was 4,423 at the 1990 census. Beginning with the 2010 census, the area was not recorded as a distinct place. While now recognized as part of Happy Valley, Sunnyside was a separate community prior to the twenty-first century. The story of this area begins with the famous busy commuter road that bears its name.

On January 6, 1876, a traveled route going from Harmony to Damascus was established as County Road #96. This road would later be named Sunnyside Road.[82] Almost one hundred years later, it was ordered by the Board of Clackamas County Commissioners that all roads within the Clackamas Post Office service area have the prefix "Southeast" added to their names. It became effective on March 22, 1972, and Sunnyside Road became Southeast Sunnyside Road.[83] For much of its history, Sunnyside

Looking west along Sunnyside Road from about 139th Avenue in 1989. The Ed Ott barn is seen at left. *Bud Unruh.*

Road was not the busy commuter route that it became by the end of the twentieth century. Louis Ott, a Sunnyside resident who was born there in 1910, later recalled that when he was a boy, "you were lucky to see a couple of cars drive by a day" on the dirt and gravel Sunnyside Road. During winter, when the snow was so deep that the road was no longer passable, it would close for two weeks, and the locals had to use shovels to clear it of the fallen flakes.[84] Where Sunnyside Road crosses over Mount Scott Creek, Sunnyside residents would simply go down through the creek using their horses and wagons. But when the first vehicles arrived, a bridge was needed. A doctor's car became stuck in the creek after he helped deliver local newborn Iva Hubbard. Horses were able to pull his car from the water.[85] In June 1912, a new steel bridge over Mount Scott Creek was constructed, and it would become known as the Sunnyside Bridge.[86]

One of the early settlers of the Sunnyside area was Seth Johnson, who settled there in the 1870s.[87] He came to Oregon in 1873 and worked as a carpenter in Portland. Johnson donated land for the Sunnyside Pioneer Cemetery, which is located along 132nd Avenue just north of Sunnyside Road. His wife Lydia's father, William Comstock, was the first person to be buried there in 1882. Susanna Reed, Seth's second daughter, and her husband were among the heirs who later donated the cemetery property to

The Sunnyside Pioneer Cemetery along 132nd Avenue north of Sunnyside Road. *Happy Valley History Collection.*

the Sunnyside Pioneer Cemetery Association.[88] Seth Johnson died in 1911 after being partially paralyzed the last five years of his life and was buried in the cemetery.

The Sunnyside Post Office was established on December 17, 1888, with John R. Welch as postmaster.[89] The office was located at the corner of Sunnyside Road and Hunters Lane, which was the name for 132nd Avenue north of Sunnyside Road. Members of the Hunter family, after whom Hunters Lane was named, are buried in the Sunnyside Pioneer Cemetery.[90] The office closed on August 12, 1903, likely because of the extension of rural free delivery.

The northwest corner of 132nd Avenue and Sunnyside Road was the property of the Ott family, who operated a general store and feed mill, and it was considered the commerce center for the community. Frank Ott, who came to Oregon from Wisconsin in 1890, built a new mill warehouse in 1908.[91] The upper floor of the warehouse would also be used as a dance hall. Alongside the warehouse, Ott built a blacksmith shop for farmers to do their horseshoeing, a barbershop and a pool hall. In 1912, he held a grand opening for his general store that would be known as the Sunnyside Country Store.[92] His wife, Louise, ran the store, and they sold everything needed in the area, including drills, plows, nails, flour and livestock feed.[93] After the store and mill were later repurposed into other businesses, the property became known as Sunnyside Commons. Mary Ott Piper, Frank Ott's granddaughter, helped preserve these and other historic buildings.[94]

Across the street from the Ott property is the Sunnyside Grange Hall. The grange was built in a Vernacular architectural style in 1920.[95] The hall was considered the social center of the Sunnyside community, with farmers holding meetings there; 4-H groups also met there, and the local residents would celebrate Christmas there. Mary Ott Piper's grandfather John Lorenz played Santa Claus for many years, and the local kids also performed a Christmas pageant at the hall.[96] The grange was designated a Clackamas County Historic Landmark in 1991. At that time, Sunnyside Road was part of a road-widening project by the county. Thanks to the efforts of Sunnyside residents and the county government, the grange was moved farther away from the road so the building could be saved from demolition and Sunnyside Road could proceed with expansion.[97]

The Sunnyside Country Store in 1978. *Clackamas County Historical Society.*

The section of 132nd Avenue south of Sunnyside Road was previously known as Hubbard Lane.[98] Marvin Hubbard was one of the first settlers in Sunnyside when he claimed eighty acres northeast of 132nd Avenue. He cut railroad ties for a living, and he and his wife, Emily, later moved to a home on 122nd Avenue and Sunnyside Road, which later became the site of a gas station. Marvin's son Walter Hubbard farmed along Hubbard Lane.[99] Walter was a lifelong resident of Sunnyside, and he married Alma Kunze in 1911.[100] Alma was born in 1890 in Germany to Frederick and Lena Kunze, who had eight children together. After the Kunze family immigrated to the United States, they lived in Vancouver, Washington. Alma's brother Carl visited a cutlery store in Portland owned by Ed Ott's sister Ida. Carl mentioned he had a sister who was looking for a job. Ida said her brother owned a farm and could use someone for housework. One of the people working for Ed, who would have a notable big red barn on his property along Sunnyside Road, was Walter Hubbard. Hubbard didn't speak German, and Alma didn't speak English. Despite this, they became friends and taught each other words in their different languages. They eventually fell in love and married. Walter wrote in his journal that the difference between bachelor and married life was the sixty-one pounds he gained in weight in a short amount of time.[101] Walter and Alma Hubbard would have twelve children together: Iva, Opal, Juanita (Nita), Vernon, Edna, Lloyd, Wallace (Wally), Ruth, Howard, Leona, a boy who died at birth and Wilbur (Bill).[102] On the Hubbard farm, all the kids pitched in and worked hard. The family raised berries and cucumbers on several acres. Like other families in the Sunnyside and Happy Valley area, farming was their livelihood.[103] Cherries and raspberries were also plentiful in the area, and locals would preserve them by canning. In 1906, Sunnyside Road–area farmers were getting six to eight cents a pound for their raspberries.[104]

Adolf Gutknecht, a German-speaking immigrant born in Russia, became another notable resident. He was born in 1885 and came to the United States in 1909. Gutknecht came to Sunnyside and owned and operated a small tannery near 126th Avenue and Sunnyside Road beginning in 1928. He tanned hides for people who came from miles around and also made leather shoestrings.[105] Adolf and his wife, Olga, had two daughters named Ida and Evelyn. Fred Hurse, Ida's husband, worked with his father-in-law at the tannery and took over the business in 1950 after Adolf retired. Hurse operated the tannery until 1965.[106] Gutknecht died in 1964 while vacationing in Tijuana, Mexico, and was buried at Lincoln Memorial Park.[107]

A man named William Donley did much of the logging in Sunnyside by axe. When early settlers arrived at Sunnyside, old-growth timber was considered trash timber. The trees were too large to be of use, so they were burned and their roots were removed so the land could be farmed. Any logs that were considered workable were cut and brought to the Lents district in Portland to be sold.[108]

At the northeast corner of 122nd Avenue and Sunnyside Road was the Sunnyside School, which opened in 1884. Children from the valley bowl also attended this school before moving to their own schoolhouse in the bowl in 1892. Sunnyside students used this school until 1949, when the new Sunnyside Elementary School opened. The old Sunnyside School, which was also used for church services by the Sunnyside Community Church, was purchased by the church and later demolished.[109] The congregation built a new building for its church, and it served as an ideal location along Sunnyside Road when the community was a rural area. However, this changed when new residential developments and businesses were built along the road and began to cause traffic problems. When Clackamas County expanded the road, the church's parking lot and driveway were sacrificed. The county offered to purchase the church property, but an agreement could not be reached until the two sides went to court in 2002. One year later, the dispute was settled, and Clackamas County paid the church $1.1 million. The congregation worshiped at the Oregon Institute of Technology along Harmony Road until a new building along Highway 212 in Damascus was dedicated in 2005.[110] The church building was demolished by the county, but the concrete foundation was left behind to control erosion. That corner of the intersection then became an unflattering site littered by trash and graffiti. As an estimated fifteen thousand vehicles passed by that spot each day in the early 2010s, a local moms club asked the City of Happy Valley to change it into something more eye-pleasing. City councilor Tom Andrusko led a project to clean up the corner and build a new city monument sign. The city purchased the property from the county and built the Happy Valley monument welcoming travelers along Sunnyside Road in 2013.[111]

When you drive eastward past the Happy Valley monument and past the historic center of the Sunnyside community at 132nd Avenue continuing along Sunnyside Road, you reach the eastern limits of the City of Happy Valley at 172nd Avenue. Here was the center of a neighborhood along Sunnyside Road known as the Rock Creek community. On April 20, 1997, the Rock Creek Community Hall hosted old-timers and descendants of Happy Valley and

Students at the Sunnyside School in 1943. *Clackamas County Historical Society.*

Sunnyside-area pioneers to celebrate and recognize the people who created these communities. The community hall on 172nd Avenue was built in 1920 with wood cut from the William Monner sawmill, which was located just off 162nd Avenue near Monner Road.[112] As in the valley bowl and at Sunnyside, the Rock Creek area was farmland and mostly undeveloped until the late twentieth century. The stream Rock Creek flows through this area, and the secluded Rock Creek Falls, located just east of 152nd Avenue, served as a hidden retreat for local kids from farm and schoolwork.[113] An unfortunate story of a family at Rock Creek was shared in the *Oregon City Enterprise* in June 1906. It read:

> *A little story is told of a man in our neighborhood, who having a twenty dollar gold piece gave it to his wife to put away. She thought first to hide*

it under the carpet, but finally put it in the coffee pot. The girls, wishing to make coffee for dinner put coffee in and after dinner threw out the grounds. After a while the man commenced to inquire for the money; the wife remembered and the hunt began. It has not been reported whether it has been found or not.[114]

Also at the corner of 172nd Avenue and Sunnyside Road was the Rock Creek schoolhouse. It was built on property owned by Alice and George Deardorff, who leased it to the Rock Creek School District. The school was later rented and purchased by a church group, and the building became the Emmanuel Community Church.[115] Down 172nd Avenue south of the school and community hall was the Hazelfern Dairy near Rock Creek Boulevard. The dairy's long once cream-colored barn was built in 1930 and became one of the last surviving historical barns in the Happy Valley area when others were dismantled.[116]

Early Happy Valley and Sunnyside people shared a common history with their communities consisting of farmlands and mostly undeveloped land. By the 1990s, a surge of housing and business developments ended a rivalry of sorts between the neighborhoods. In 1997, Eva Ulrich Ott, a longtime resident of both the valley and Sunnyside, shared that for a time Sunnyside people didn't like Happy Valley people that much, and Happy Valley residents felt the same about Sunnyside residents. Other than the pioneer days when people from the valley attended school and church at Sunnyside until getting their own, residents from the two neighborhoods didn't mix together that much. Some Sunnyside community residents would refer to their neighbors to the north who they had conflicts or quarreled with as living in "Skunk Hollow." Despite this animosity between the two, whether it be playful or serious, several Happy Vallians and Sunnysiders shared relations, as in the case of Eva Ulrich marrying Louis Ott of Sunnyside.[117]

Another commonality of Sunnyside and Happy Valley people was living in a close, tightknit community. Ron Orme, who served as principal at both Sunnyside and Happy Valley Elementary Schools, said that when he moved to the Sunnyside area in the early 1960s, everybody was familiar and pretty much knew everybody else. "Sunnyside was a place where you could go out on a bike or a horse, wave to everybody and everyone knew everyone who lived up and down the street. The neighbors of Sunnyside were a really happy, very connected group of people who loved visiting with one another," he said.[118] Although it is no longer a distinct census-designated place and became identified with the City of Happy Valley, the community of Sunnyside has maintained its identity as a neighborhood of happy people who love living on the sunny side of the mountain.

Chapter 6

THE OTTS

A Sunnyside Family

The northwest corner of 132nd Avenue and Sunnyside Road is a significant location in local history. You will see two buildings that look like something from an Old West town that have been used as a gift shop and a restaurant. These structures were originally used as a country store and feed mill and are located on property formerly owned by Frank Ott and his family. This site was considered the commerce center for the Sunnyside community and was frequently visited by residents of the Happy Valley area. To tell the story of this historic Sunnyside family, we begin with how the Otts came to Oregon and Sunnyside, as presented here from the writings of Frank Ott in 1959. He wrote:

> *Frank Ott's father Florian was born in 1842. After the 1838 German Revolution, Florian's family moved from Bavaria, Germany to Austria. Florian's mother Alexa Ritterch's family owned a large farm in Austria and that's where Florian was born. Florian and his family departed for America from Bremen, Germany. When they arrived at New York they knew no one and couldn't speak English. They eventually settled in Mishicot, Wisconsin and lived on a homestead with horses, cattle and sheep. When Frank was three years old his mother died in childbirth. A couple of years later Florian remarried to a woman named Katie Schmidt. Frank felt his stepmother was a good mother to her own children but not to him as she always put him to work and would never let him play as a kid. In 1890, Florian sold the farm and they moved to Oregon. The*

year before, Florian's son, Ambrose, who had moved to Oregon and built a sawmill, was murdered. Florian left to settle his son's estate and when he returned he liked Oregon so much he decided to sell his farm and move the family there. It took them six days to travel by train to Oregon. After reaching Portland, the plan was to continue south to Lane County where Florian had a farm already picked out. However, Katie did not want to go any farther and didn't want to live on a farm anymore. So Florian rented a house in Portland. Frank got a job in a box and stave factory for one dollar a day. He was 15. Florian realized he was not a city man and in the fall of 1890 he moved the family to Sunnyside. In the spring they planted strawberries and sweet peas. They also had a prune orchard. In his early 20s, Frank walked to Portland to work and live. When he was 26 he returned to Sunnyside and paid $200 to his father for twelve acres. At that time his stepbrother Ed was being paid to help run the farm. After Ed married he bought the Ott farm from Florian who later moved to Portland and died in 1923. Frank worked for a lumber company east of Eugene and then to California and worked several other jobs. He returned to Oregon in 1899. He worked at sawmills at Rainier and then Boring before getting a job as a foreman on a farm at Rock Creek. Now that he was working close to his twelve acre property he began building. He first built a barn and then a cabin. He quit his job and became his own boss. He had no horse but his brother Ed plowed for him to raise crop. Frank planted two acres of berries, two acres of potatoes, and the rest in wheat, oats and hay. He built a grist mill so the farmers around could ground their grain in winter. Then Frank and Ed bought a threshing machine, the first gas engine to thresh grain west of the Rockies. With his place being off the main road he decided to buy a place along Sunnyside Road to build a bigger building for his mill. He then met a lady named Louise Rabbits and thought she was the finest and most honorable lady he had ever met. A year after they married he sold his 12 acres and built a new mill at his new place along Sunnyside Road. He then built a two-story warehouse where the upper floor was used as a dance hall. Alongside the warehouse he built a blacksmith shop for farmers to do their horse shoeing. Next to that was a barber shop and a pool hall. One of the buildings he used as a general store where he sold everything from a pin to a drill to a plow. His wife ran the store while Frank ran the rest. His wife died suddenly in 1923 when their sons Frank Jr., Louis and Carl were still children. After that Frank closed the dance hall as he couldn't stand anymore music and dancing.[119]

Louise Ott, wife of Frank and mother of Frank Jr., Louis and Carl Ott. *Mary Ott Piper.*

Frank Ott at age ninety-three. *Mary Ott Piper.*

In 1908, Frank Ott built a two-story warehouse for his mill, featuring a dance hall on the upper floor.[120] He then built a storage building for his feed mill in 1910. Frank would grind feed for the neighbors until midnight.[121] After a short time, Ott realized that in addition to supplying feed and grain to the community, he could also supply groceries and other necessities. He transformed the storage building adjacent to the warehouse into a general store and held a grand opening and dance on May 25, 1912.[122] At Ott's dance hall, people would dance in groups and perform the Virginia reel.[123] In the decades the Sunnyside Country Store was open, the store sold an array of items, including soda, beer, dry goods, snacks, milk, pails, shirts, boots and so much more.[124] Frank operated the general store and feed mill until 1935.[125] His son Carl then owned the country store and feed mill and also fixed tractors for the neighbors. Carl's daughter Mary then inherited the property.[126] Mary Ott Piper wanted to make sure the buildings her grandfather built would survive into the future. After the store and mill had been repurposed into other businesses, she persuaded Clackamas County to designate her family's historic structures as Sunnyside Commons.[127] She was also successful in relocating other historic structures to the Commons site, including the 1890 Zinser family home from the valley bowl and the Arthur Mather home from Clackamas that was built in the 1890s. Mather's home, post office and general store were for many years the center of the Clackamas community. Some of the businesses that have operated at Sunnyside Commons include DG Wine Cellar, Sunnyside Mercantile Antiques, Home Again Antiques, Sublime Clothing and Gloria'z Pub and Grill.[128]

One of the area's historic buildings that was dismantled was the barn of Ed Ott. Although Frank Ott referred to him as his stepbrother, Ed was Frank's half brother. Ed purchased property along Sunnyside Road from their father, Florian. Ott's towering red barn was located just east of

132nd Avenue. It is unknown exactly when the barn was constructed, but the Clackamas County Cultural Resource Inventory in 1984 listed the construction date as about 1930.[129] Ed owned the barn until 1957. Despite being on the county's inventory of historic buildings, it was not enough to save it from being removed to make way for the widening of Sunnyside Road. At the time, the road was two lanes, one going in each direction, and congestion urged the need for expansion. The Sunnyside Road landmark stood until 2005, when it was one of the last remaining historical barns in the Happy Valley area.[130]

Frank Ott passed away at age ninety-eight in 1974 and was buried in the Sunnyside Pioneer Cemetery. In addition to the mill and store he opened, Frank was also remembered for bringing the first gas-powered threshing machine to Oregon, being an organizer of the first telephone system in Oregon and being a special deputy in Sunnyside for many years.[131] Frank Ott and his family provided so much to the Sunnyside community. Anyone could go to the Ott property to get everything from grain to feed, from a haircut to horseshoes, from groceries to a new pair of boots and even be entertained by playing pool or going dancing. If one ever drives by or visits the intersection of 132nd Avenue and Sunnyside Road, always remember the family who helped make this neighborhood an ideal place to live.

Chapter 7

RURAL AND BEAUTIFUL

Building a Unique Town

At the beginning of the twentieth century, Happy Valley's identity was that of an isolated, rural, widely unknown farming settlement. It mostly stayed that way until the 1990s, when it began to become known as an urban, rapidly developing community of residences and growth. But before Happy Valley could become the steadily expanding city of rooftops that it did by the end of the century, the community would need several conveniences that it lacked—such as paved roads, electricity, fire protection and more.

When Happy Valley was just a farming settlement and consisted of only a spacious valley sequestered between the slopes of Mount Scott and Scouters Mountain, the first roads were dirt trails carved by farm wagons.[132] The Happy Valley Elementary School students in 1969 learned from interviews with old-timers that dusty summers and muddy winters made Happy Valley roads rough to traverse even after they were graveled. For road building in Happy Valley, locals used horse-drawn slip scrapers and shovels to remove dirt and dynamite to blast away tree stumps.[133] Some roads had logs laid across them side by side covered with dirt to make a steep road more passable by helping wagons and eventually the first cars from slipping down the wet road. These corduroy roads were used to travel over Mount Scott.

The road that became known as Mount Scott Boulevard started out as a wagon-carved trail that was eventually graded and for a time was known as Deardorff Road. By about 1915, the northern half was named Mount Scott Boulevard and the southern half, from Ridgecrest down to King Road, was

A horse team using a slip scraper in Happy Valley in 1915. *Clackamas County Historical Society.*

called Zinser Road, named after the family who lived in the area.[134] Resident Herman Kanne described the valley in 1912 as having "two main roads out of the valley, one leading northwesterly to Lents and the other north to what is known as Foster road; also one leading to Sunnyside, one and a half miles south. Our roads are being improved rapidly and it will only be a matter of a few years until all of our roads are graveled. We have formed a road district and so are enabled to help ourselves in this matter."[135]

By the end of the nineteenth century, Happy Valley residents wanted a more level, or at least a less steep, road to pass going northward to Portland. William Albert Deardorff, John M. Deardorff's son, worked from the family farm delivering grain and produce to Portland by a horse-drawn wagon. The precipitous route over Mount Scott inspired the Deardorff family and local resident C.W. Gay to persuade Multnomah and Clackamas County commissioners to improve a route going north to Foster Road so products could be more easily delivered to markets. A survey was conducted in 1898 with John Bennett Deardorff as one of the axe men to lay out a new county road.[136] A new bridge was constructed spanning Johnson Creek, replacing an earlier bridge built in 1885. This bridge, later named Cedar Creek Crossing, would be replaced in 1936 and again in 1982.[137] The road was named Deardorff Road (not to be confused with Mount Scott Boulevard, which was also known by that name for a time). While this road is called Deardorff Road on the Multnomah County side, it is known as 132nd Avenue on the Clackamas County side. It was also known as "Snake Road" by locals because of its many winding turns.[138] 132nd Avenue, with part of King Road, and 129th Avenue down to the Sunnyside School at the corner of Sunnyside Road and 122nd Avenue would be designated by Clackamas County to be a market road known as Market Road Number 29.[139] This market road was declared by the county court led by Judge Harvey Cross in 1922 so market road funds could be used for its improvement.[140]

Over the years, Clackamas County made improvements to the roads in Happy Valley, with the first paved road completed in 1925.[141] After roads were improved, people from Portland and other nearby places would take leisurely car rides through the valley, as it made for an ideal afternoon drive. In 1927, one of these recreational drivers, Ernest W. Peterson, called the trip through Happy Valley a "beautiful drive" and in detail wrote:

I saw swollen streams, green fields, fruit trees in full bloom, others just budding out, pussy willows, beautiful valleys with small streams coursing through them, stock grazing in the fields and happy school children playing in the school yards. But the best part of the drive was the rest of body and mind which it brought.[142]

In 1908, a telephone line was installed, providing valley residents telecommunication with the outside world for the first time. With the Bell call system, calls went to an operator at the Mount Scott Drugstore in Lents who would then connect the caller with the person and city they wanted to reach.[143] Electricity came to Happy Valley in 1925. It was a memorable event because it occurred leading up to the Christmas season and the residents were able to use electric lights on their trees rather than candles.[144]

Logging aided Happy Valley in its development as a community. One man in particular who contributed much of the logging in the area was William Monner. He operated a sawmill site at 162nd Avenue, and most of the logging took place from 147th Avenue down to Hagen Road in Pleasant Valley, an area located east of Scouters Mountain stretching across the boundary between Clackamas and Multnomah Counties.[145] Monner also did some logging on Scouters Mountain and in the Happy Valley bowl. The area was mostly woods when Monner and his family came there. The Monner family cleared out Douglas fir trees in the early 1930s. Monner built his sawmill with his brother-in-law and employed about six or seven people. Jobs at the mill included hauling logs and cutting lumber. The employees lived in cabins at the site, and their wages ranged between twenty and fifty cents an hour. A horse team would haul between one and four logs at a time, which ranged between one and four feet thick. A boiler and two engines were used to cut the timbers inside the mill. Lumberyards purchased the lumber and hauled it away in trucks. After the mill burned down, the property was sold. Clackamas County then built and named Monner Road after him. After William Monner retired as the sawmill operator, he died in a Milwaukie hospital after a brief illness in 1972.[146]

A significant piece to Happy Valley's development was a water system. In 1930, the Mount Scott Water District was officially incorporated by the State of Oregon.[147] In 1931, the district's first reservoir was built on Mount Scott, and water pipes were installed.[148] After World War II, in about 1946, with farmland being divided and sold off, a central water system began supplying water to new homes.[149] Prior to the Mount Scott District, people depended on wells and cisterns for water. A small building at the corner of King Road and 129th Avenue became the home for the water district office and would also host the City of Happy Valley staff before the first city hall was built across the street. In 2000, the Mount Scott Water District merged with the Damascus Water District to establish the Sunrise Water Authority.[150] The Water Authority provides drinking water to residents of Happy Valley, Damascus and parts of unincorporated Clackamas County.

William Monner's sawmill in 1925. *Clackamas County Historical Society.*

In order to protect Happy Valley from fire disasters as it developed, organized firefighting would be needed. In 1949, Happy Valley Fire District #65 was formed by volunteers to serve the community. The district later annexed the Sunnyside and Rock Creek areas. In the beginning, four-wheel-drive trucks, a Ford at the home of Donald Meng and a Chevy at the home of Ed Rebstock were used by volunteering residents to fight fires.[151] In 1954, the first fire chief was appointed. William Beutler, also known as "Bill," and his wife, Shirley, bought property on Mount Scott in the early 1950s. After he inquired about Happy Valley's fire protection district, he soon found himself volunteering as a firefighter and being appointed the community's first fire chief despite having no firefighting experience.[152] In case of an emergency, a siren, which was mounted on a pole at the Meng property, would sound the alarm when a fire call was made. With many of the men working out the valley, Chief Beutler trained several women to drive the trucks and operate the water pumps. Shirley Beutler, Erma Rebstock and Lois Costine rotated as dispatchers, and each had a button they would press at their homes to sound the alarm when a fire call came in. They also made sure one of them would always be home in case of a call. In 1956, the fire department began sponsoring a Fourth of July fireworks show to raise funds for firefighting equipment. The firefighting volunteers went door to door collecting donations and then put on a fireworks show for the community.[153] The July 4th show became an event that attracted visitors from outside the valley and grew over the years into the biggest event of the year in the city.

In 1957, a groundbreaking took place to pour a concrete foundation for a fire station building. In 1958, the community came together to help in the construction of the Happy Valley Fire Station at the corner of King Road and 129th Avenue. Being an engineer, Chief William Beutler designed the station. Construction of the building would not be completed for several years as the second-story portion of the station would not be constructed until the late 1960s.[154] Beutler served as the volunteer fire chief for more than eleven years before stepping down and died from a heart defect in 1967.[155] In 1988, Happy Valley Fire District #65 merged with Clackamas County Fire District #54 and Clackamas Fire District #71 following concerns over future tax-base losses caused by annexation of property by surrounding jurisdictions.[156] Other mergers over the years led to Clackamas Fire District #1 serving and protecting citizens across north Clackamas County, with stations in the Happy Valley area along King Road, Causey Avenue and 172nd Avenue.

Happy Valley's first fire chief, William "Bill" Beutler. *Mike Beutler.*

The Happy Valley Fire Station in 1996. *Bud Unruh.*

Across the road southwest of the fire station is where Happy Valley's first church was built. In 1891, what would become known as the Happy Valley Evangelical Church was constructed and consisted of just one room. Before the church was built, the valley's Christian disciples went to Sunnyside or Rock Creek for worship. As there was no pastor who lived in the valley, a minister from Lents would walk over Mount Scott to preach in the church every Sunday. In 1912, resident Herman Kanne described the church as being "well attended by the community."[157] The original building was torn down and replaced by a larger one that was built in 1915. The third church building was built in 1947 with a pastor's residence next to it.[158] It was also called the Happy Valley Evangelical United Brethren and later changed its name to Happy Valley Community Church.

Due to the strong determination from locals in the valley bowl and Mount Scott to maintain and preserve the area as a farming community, businesses like a gas station, barbershop or grocery store never opened in the Happy Valley bowl. The people saw no need for commercialism in their valley. When resident Noreen Sample first saw Happy Valley in 1920, she experienced and fell in love with the uniqueness of a town that consisted only of farms and houses. She wrote, "[This] was my first impression of Happy Valley—wild, lonely, intensely quiet—beautiful. And over it all was an aura of peace."[159]

The people wanted to keep their rural, beautiful and unique town free of commercialism. For a long time, when looking over the valley all one would see were farms, a scattering of houses, a church for worship and a school near its center. Although Happy Valley would later expand its borders to include retail establishments and businesses within its city limits and the farms were replaced with more homes and trees, the bowl remains a reminder of what the pioneers and farmers wanted their little community town to be—a beautiful place to live.

Chapter 8

A LESSON IN EDUCATION

Happy Valley Area Schools

D id you ever go to a school where the students of every grade met in one room and had one teacher? Did you ever go to a school where you had to carry a pail, walk to a nearby spring, fill it with water and carry it back to class so your schoolmates could have drinking water? Were you ever in a school where in addition to learning about reading, writing and arithmetic, you also had to clean out the ashes from a wood furnace? This is what it was like for the children of the Happy Valley area when it was a farming community.

Prior to the construction of the first school in the bowl, the children of the valley had to go to Sunnyside or Rock Creek for schooling. But in 1891, John Bennett Deardorff donated an acre of land from his father John M. Deardorff's land claim for a schoolhouse. A small one-room building with a steeple opened in 1892. It was the same location where the Happy Valley Elementary School would later be constructed along King Road. It would be called the Christilla School, a combination of the names of Christian and Matilda Deardorff. John Bennett Deardorff, the school district's clerk, got a large bell made that was placed in the steeple and could be heard throughout the valley. Rachel Deardorff, John Bennett's mother, made the first American flag for the school.[160]

In interviews with old-timers by the Happy Valley Elementary School students in 1969, the original schoolhouse was described as containing two small cloakrooms near the front door. The teacher's desk stood on a raised platform with the students' desks situated in two rows leaving a center aisle. A large wood stove in the center of the building provided heat when needed. Behind the schoolhouse were two outdoor toilets, one for boys and one for girls. Also on the grounds were homemade seesaws for playground equipment.[161] At recess, the students would play ring toss, ball games, Skip to My Lou and tag in the woods nearby. For the school to have water, two students carried a pail southward to a spring that flowed down from Scouters Mountain. The water was poured into a jar with a faucet, and each kid had their own individual cup. Girls usually wore full skirts and sweaters while attending class.[162]

In the beginning, one teacher taught all eight grades in the single-room schoolhouse, and the number of students averaged about forty. The first teacher was Mr. Lonnie Brooks, who taught for one year.[163] The teacher would also do the janitorial work of sweeping and general cleaning.[164] In 1917, the original school building was torn down and replaced by a larger one with a basement containing a wood-burning furnace. For older students, it was part of their schoolwork to put wood into the furnace and clean out the ashes.[165] The school was renamed the East Mount Scott School. By this time, the schoolhouse was using a twelve-foot-deep cistern for water.[166] The Deardorff bell was removed from the steeple and placed on a wooden pedestal outside the new one-room school. In the 1960s, the bell was stolen from the pedestal. While it was being investigated by Clackamas County deputies, Happy Valley resident Virginia Zinser spotted the bell lying along Deardorff Road. She got two of her sons to load it into her car, and the bell was returned to the school.[167] The bell hung from a brick pedestal outside the elementary school for many years. In 2008, after the old elementary building was torn down, the bell was placed in a new spot on display outside the entrance to the new Happy Valley Elementary School building.

In 1936, a wing containing a stage was added, with more classrooms built over the years.[168] After other classrooms were added, the old 1917 one-room schoolhouse was used as the library. When a new library was added on, the room became vacant.[169] When this author went to Happy Valley Elementary in the 1990s, the old one-room schoolhouse was used as the music room. In 1954, East Mount Scott School patrons voted thirty-four to three to change the name of the school to Happy Valley School.[170] In 1960, the large brick building of the elementary school was constructed, and in 1967, the north section containing the fifth- and sixth-grade classrooms was built.[171] In 1969, the school published *The History of Happy Valley, Oregon* as a project researched and completed by the grade school students.

The Happy Valley Elementary School as it appeared in the 1970s. *Happy Valley History Collection.*

Reading, writing and arithmetic were the usual things younglings would learn in Happy Valley's first schoolhouses, which was known as District #99.[172] For Arbor Day, the school kids dug up flower beds and planted flowers. A special event the students did every year was present a program for the community. Each grade would present their own part following weeks of preparation by the teacher, and the students would wear costumes made by their mothers. Erma Rebstock made a clown suit for her son Karl for one program. These programs would be attended by a standing room–only crowd, and the school program was considered one of the biggest days of the year in the town.[173] Another big day of the year happened near the end of the school year when the Happy Valley School students walked over to the Sunnyside School to play a ballgame against the Sunnyside students. That was considered a big deal for the kids.[174]

For decades, prior to school buses, all students had to walk to the schoolhouse. In their walk to the one-room school, some Happy Valley–area kids used karo syrup buckets as lunch pails.[175] In a 1997 interview, resident Eva Ulrich Ott explained that when she went to school in Happy Valley, the kids walked a mile to the schoolhouse and it was quite a chore to walk there when it rained or snowed. The school during her childhood never closed because of snow.[176] Whenever inclement snowy weather occurred, it was the only time the kids were given transportation by use of a horse or sleigh ride.[177] Snow would cancel school by the time buses became available in the area due to the dangerous weather conditions. Although winter's snow and ice are not as bad as they used to be, the North Clackamas School

District would determine whether to close schools based on snow conditions in Happy Valley due to its landscape of steep hills and slopes.[178]

Due to the city's booming population growth, the Happy Valley School would need to grow too. By 2008, twelve portable classrooms were in use at the overcrowded Happy Valley Elementary School. Thanks to a 2006 bond to renovate and build new schools in the North Clackamas School District, the old Happy Valley Elementary School was torn down in the summer of 2008 and replaced with a new building. In the fall, students moved into their new school built on the same grounds as the earlier Happy Valley schools.[179]

Prior to the opening of the first school in the Happy Valley bowl, settlers to the south in the Sunnyside Road area had a one-room school built for area children in 1884. That year, a man with the last name Walfe, or possibly Wolfe, donated a portion of his property on the northeast corner of Happy Hollow Road (later renamed 122nd Avenue) and Sunnyside Road to be used for a school. Local farmers with horses and slip scrapers graded the hillside to level the ground. The Sunnyside School was known as Sunnyside School District #71. The front door faced Sunnyside Road, with a stove inside for heat. Also on the school grounds were two outhouses, a cistern for water and a woodshed.[180] The school's cistern had a problem with snakes and mice

The Sunnyside School at the corner of 122nd Avenue and Sunnyside Road. *Happy Valley History Collection.*

always getting into it. The students apparently didn't mind, though, and they used a bucket to pull water out for everybody to drink. They used the cistern until the school got running water from a pipe from a neighbor.[181]

In 1890, forty-five students and one teacher occupied the Sunnyside School. The opening of the Christilla School in the bowl in 1892 eased the crowding at Sunnyside for a time. By 1896, more room was needed, and a large addition was constructed for the upper grades and an additional teacher was hired to teach those students.[182] Like at the Christilla School, a bell would ring to alarm Sunnyside students when school was about to start. Also similar to the school in the bowl, the Sunnyside School bell was stolen by persons unknown, and unfortunately, this one was never recovered.[183] The 1930s brought several improvements to the Sunnyside School, including electricity, a basement that was dug by Works Progress Administration workers, a furnace to replace the wood-burning stove and running water from a pipe. In 1944, Sunnyside-area women started a hot lunch program for the school by canning, cooking and fundraising. Also that year, the Sunnyside Parent Teacher Association was organized.[184]

By 1949, attendance was outgrowing and crowding the small Sunnyside School. The school board needed to construct a brand-new school elsewhere to accommodate the increasing student enrollment and selected property owned by Charley Hunter on Hubbard Lane (later renamed 132nd Avenue) and Sunnyside Road for a new school. In April 1949, ground was broken and a four-room school with an office, library and restrooms was built. Classes started in the fall, and a dedication ceremony for the new Sunnyside Elementary School took place on November 10. The old school, which was also used for Sunday school and church services, was purchased by the Sunnyside Community Church and was demolished.[185]

On January 9, 1952, a fire caused extensive damage to Sunnyside Elementary. Classes were moved temporarily to the Sunnyside Grange Hall next door until repairs could be made. In March, enough repairs were completed for students to return to the school building. In 1954, a new gym was added. In 1956, the Sunnyside School District consolidated with Milwaukie schools, and the following year, the seventh and eighth graders began attending Dale Ickes Junior High School along Harmony Road in Milwaukie. In 1960, about five acres were purchased from the Mortenson family to build additional classrooms for the elementary school. In 1979, another unit consisting of an office, a library and four classrooms was constructed.[186] The year 1979 also saw the inclusion of a kindergarten class at Sunnyside for the first time.[187] The school underwent a major renovation project that was completed in 2019. The renovations included additional classroom space, seismic and technology upgrades, a new covered student waiting area and an expanded cafeteria and courtyard.[188]

To the east of the Sunnyside School along Sunnyside Road where it meets 172nd Avenue was the schoolhouse for the Rock Creek School District #31. Alice and George Deardorff donated land for the school to serve the Rock Creek community.[189] George was the son of David Deardorff, who owned a donation land claim at Rock Creek where the schoolhouse would be built. David was a son of Christian and Matilda Deardorff, the first settlers in Happy Valley. The school was built sometime in the early 1900s and became a cornerstone of the Rock Creek area.[190] In 1906, the Rock Creek School had thirty-one students and would hold plays and ice cream socials to benefit the schoolhouse.[191] After the Rock Creek School District consolidated with the Clackamas School District, the school remained empty for about two years. A church group then started renting the building from the district and later purchased the old school from them. Although renovations were made to the building, it structurally remained the same into the twenty-first century as the Emmanuel Community Church.[192]

In the 1920s, Happy Valley, Sunnyside and Rock Creek joined other school districts in north Clackamas County to create a unified high school district to

The Rock Creek School at the corner of 172nd Avenue and Sunnyside Road in 1909. *Wilmer Gardner Research Library.*

provide a close-to-home option for students wanting higher education after grammar school. Union High School District #5 was formed by a vote of the people from the districts involved on February 28, 1925. The new high school district was composed of the grammar school districts of Milwaukie, Concord, Rock Creek, Harmony, Battin, Clackamas, East Clackamas, Sunnyside, Happy Valley (known then as East Mount Scott), Oak Grove and Wichita. A bond election held on May 9, 1925, passed, and the construction of a new high school building commenced. The new Union High School in Milwaukie, which Happy Valley area students would attend, was dedicated on September 3, 1926. By 1971, North Clackamas residents sought a single unified district of all schools to bring more efficient administration, save money and provide a better-quality education for all. Voters approved the creation of the North Clackamas School District, and the adoption of a final plan for administrative school district #12 was approved by the Clackamas County District Boundary Board on September 20, 1971. Going forward, this new school district would make decisions regarding schools in the Happy Valley area.

Happy Valley–area students attended the Milwaukie High School until the Union High School District opened Clackamas High School on Webster Road near Milwaukie. It was dedicated on November 14, 1957, and had fewer than seven hundred students when it opened.[193] On April 3, 2002, a new building for Clackamas High School students opened on 122nd Avenue in Clackamas.[194] The opening was delayed from an original opening date in 2001 because the building wasn't ready to be occupied. Almost immediately after the new school opened, portable classrooms were needed to ease overcrowding due to the rapidly growing Happy Valley–area population. Eventually, the nearby Sunrise Middle School was converted into the eastern campus of the high school, and the old Clackamas High School building became Alder Creek Middle School.

Other schools to open over the years include Mount Scott Elementary School. The school on Stevens Road opened in 1989 but was unfinished, as the library lacked books and the gym floor was still being installed when the first students arrived for class.[195] A four-classroom north wing was added to Mount Scott Elementary in 1991.[196] In 2000, Spring Mountain Elementary School opened along 129th Avenue. This school was built to serve the growing population in the Happy Valley and Sunnyside area.[197] The new Spring Mountain Elementary would not be enough though to satisfy Happy Valley's rapidly growing population. Therefore, a bond was passed in 2006 to allow the North Clackamas School District to renovate and build new schools across the district. This included dismantling the old Happy Valley Elementary School and replacing it with a brand-new larger building in 2008. Adjoining the newly built elementary school was the new Happy Valley Middle School, which opened in 2009. Happy Valley's first junior high school brought some needed relief to crowding at Sunrise Middle School in Clackamas. The year 2009 also saw the opening of Scouters Mountain Elementary School, which was built to relieve crowding at Happy Valley Elementary.[198] Verne A. Duncan Elementary School opened that year as well by 172nd Avenue just north of Highway 212 in Happy Valley. This school was built to relieve crowding at Oregon Trail Elementary in Clackamas and was named after a state superintendent of public instruction and state senator in Oregon.[199] Rock Creek Middle School opened in 2010 by Rock Creek Boulevard. This building was later renovated and converted into Adrienne C. Nelson High School, which opened in 2021. Rock Creek Middle School students then relocated to a building that opened in 1991 along 132nd Avenue in Clackamas as Sunrise Middle School.[200] The building had served as the east campus of Clackamas High School before reverting back into a middle school under the Rock Creek name. Despite the success

Nelson High School when it opened in September 2021. *Happy Valley History Collection.*

of the 2006 bond to renovate and construct several new schools in Happy Valley, it would not be enough as the city's population continued to grow.

In 2019, the Beatrice Morrow Cannady Elementary School opened on Vogel Road.[201] It was the first school in the North Clackamas School District named after a woman and a person of color. Cannady was the first African American woman to graduate from law school in Oregon. She was also a cofounder of the NAACP chapter in Oregon and fought against racial discrimination in her career.[202] Up to this point, Happy Valley kids had attended high school outside the city limits, first going to Portland, then Milwaukie and then Clackamas. The time had come for the city to get its own high school, and it found funding thanks to a capital construction bond that voters approved in 2016 to convert the six-year-old Rock Creek Middle School into a larger building to serve high school students.

What proved to be more challenging than the renovation and expansion of the middle school into a high school was what the new school would be named. The North Clackamas School District board outlined criteria for its school naming committee to name the school after a local resident who was not a white man like the previous names chosen for North Clackamas schools. The naming committee recommended Oregon Supreme Court Justice Adrienne C. Nelson and former Oregon Symphony music director James DePreist as possible choices for the school name. Happy Valley City Council, however, issued a press release stating their recommendation: "The City Council is unanimous in its request to name the new high school in Happy Valley 'Happy Valley High School.'"[203] In May 2018, the school board voted four to three against the committee's recommendations for the high school name. The school district board decided against the committee's suggested names due to the strong dissenting opinions from the city and the community. However, one year later in May 2019, the school district board voted five to two to name the high school in Happy Valley after Justice Adrienne C. Nelson. This time, the board featured two new members who reversed the earlier decision.[204] Adrienne C. Nelson was appointed by Governor Ted Kulongoski to the Multnomah County Circuit Court in 2006. Nelson was then appointed to the Oregon Supreme Court in 2018, the first African American to serve on the court.[205] Justice Nelson proudly welcomed students and the community into the new Adrienne C. Nelson High School when it opened in 2021.[206] With Happy Valley making quite a name for itself through growth and expansion, it has also seen its schools grow and expand. One thing is for certain: more residents means more schools. How many more schools will become part of the city in the future? That is the question.

Chapter 9

REALTORS OR FOLKLORE? HOW DID HAPPY VALLEY GET ITS NAME?

T he origin of the name for the City of Happy Valley has been traditionally associated with a folkloric legend of community boys getting happily drunk from apple cider. One version of the story goes, "Boys from the Hollow enjoyed drinking Grandpa Deardorff's delicious apple cider before attending church services at Sunnyside and often used to arrive there singing loudly and gaily. Sunnyside dwellers were soon referring to them as 'the happy boys from the hollow,' and after a while the area became known as Happy Valley."[207]

However, other stories of the name origin have been shared over the years. In 1948, resident E.A. Knauss spoke on the naming of the community. He said, "Some fifty years ago there was a revival meeting and all the young people were so happy—they named it Happy Valley."[208] Royal Zinser, a longtime resident who was born in 1896, commented that when he was a kid, the locale was called Sleepy Hollow by "some feller who worked down the road and thought it was too dull around here." Later, the residents grew tired of the joke, and road signs were erected to read "Happy Hollow."[209] While these tales may or may not be true, why Happy Valley ultimately received its name might more plausibly belong to realtors who embraced the "happy" name.

The valley bowl of Happy Valley has had many names in its history, including Deardorff Settlement, Deardorff Valley, Happy Hollow, Christilla Valley and East Mount Scott. It was first referred to as the Deardorff Settlement and the Deardorff Valley, named after the first settler family in the area. The Happy Hollow name emerged from the folkloric story and appears as the name of the school locale on county surveyor maps in 1912 and 1926. East Mount Scott emerged from being the school name for a time during the first half of the twentieth century. In a meeting held at the valley's school in 1902, a new name was chosen for the community. An announcement read, "The pioneer settlement in Clackamas County, southeast of Mount Scott, which has been called 'Deardorff Valley' and 'Happy Hollow,' will be known hereafter as 'Christilla Valley.'"[210] The name was a combination of Christian (Chris) and Matilda (Tilla) Deardorff as a tribute to the patriarch and matriarch of the first pioneer family to settle in the valley. The community of farmers had seemingly decided on an official name for their locale, but the name "Christilla Valley" would not last for long.

The earliest known recorded uses of the name "Happy Valley" in referring to the geographic area between Mount Scott, Scouters Mountain and Sunnyside are found in classified advertisements selling acreage during the autumn of 1909.[211] This was seven years after the school meeting that decided the area would be known "hereafter as Christilla Valley." After that proclamation was made, the use of the name Christilla Valley was often paired with the more well-known Deardorff name, and the usage of

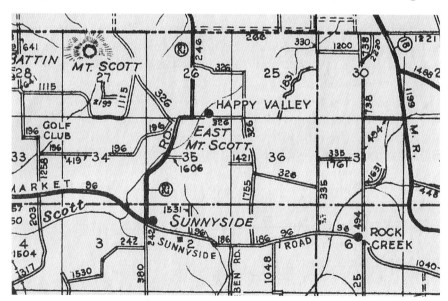

A 1948 map showing both "Happy Valley" and "East Mount Scott," two of the many names for the valley. *Wilmer Gardner Research Library.*

Happy Hollow continued as well. But despite all these different names for the same geographic area, only one has been found to be used by realtors in advertisements for selling acreage. In the classified advertisements of the *Oregonian* and Oregon City newspaper archives, the names Deardorff Settlement, Deardorff Valley, Happy Hollow, Christilla Valley and East Mount Scott are not found to be used by realtors. Only the name Happy Valley was used in selling land for that area. A simple reason could be because there was no official name for the area and the farmers living there were just notably happy people. Another explanation could lie in events that plagued the community at the start of the twentieth century.

In 1902, wildfires destroyed farmland in many parts of Clackamas County, including in the valley bowl, where resident Charles Frederick Zinser lost his house, one barn and all his grain and fences. It also took the efforts of twenty men to protect the schoolhouse from being destroyed.[212] In 1904, a severe fire approaching from Gresham posed serious danger to valley farmhouses and caused much uneasiness among the residents. An *Oregonian* article covering the fires quoted a farmer living in the valley as saying, "With a fair wind there will be little chance of saving the farmhouses," as the area was "covered with a mass of brush and dry snags and logs, which would feed a fire and carry it forward at a great rate."[213] To make things even more difficult for farmers, coyotes had invaded the area and were killing poultry and sheep. In the autumn of 1904, a hunt had to be formed of men with guns and hounds in an attempt to kill the predators. One article reported, "A large body of men armed with all sorts of shooting-sticks located the vermin, set upon them, found themselves actually attacked by the reputed cowards, and had such a case of stag fever that they pumped three hundred rounds of ammunition into the pack without hurting one."[214] With these dispiriting events occurring in the valley, realtors might have needed a clever strategy to ease the fears of future land buyers. And coincidentally, the name "Happy Valley" made an appearance in two real estate ads in 1909.

Could it be true that the name "Happy Valley" evolved from "Happy Hollow," as the legend says? Possible, but an *Oregonian* article from 1932 shows them together as two separate names. The article is a listing of various hiking locations in the Portland metro area that reads, "Happy valley—Go to Lents junction. Take road going past Mount Scott cemetery and on to Happy valley....Happy hollow—Go to Lents junction. Tramp southeasterly over Deardorf valley road to Happy hollow."[215]

If "Happy Valley" evolved from "Happy Hollow," the use of the two names here is rather odd, as they are both used to separately describe the

Overlooking the valley of many names toward Mount Scott from the Gustafsson family property in 1956. *Erik Gustafsson.*

same geographic area. An explanation for this is that these two names have different origins, one from Sunnyside with the cider-drinking legend and the other from realtors as a way of inciting optimism. Real estate developers choose names for housing areas that do not share a previous title and that would appeal to potential buyers. If early twentieth-century realtors did not want to use one of the informal names of Happy Hollow or Christilla Valley, it's possible they could have combined both to create a new name to appeal to land buyers. The formal use of the Happy Valley name did not begin until 1954, when patrons of the East Mount Scott School District voted to change the name of the schoolhouse to Happy Valley School.[216] The name stuck when the town incorporated as a municipality in 1965. Due to Happy Valley having so many different and unofficial names in its early history, its final name likely emerged from use by realtors who first used it in real estate advertisements, and interestingly, it was the only title used in identifying the valley area despite all its other more commonly known names.

Chapter 10

ED REBSTOCK AND LIVING IN
A CLOSE-KNIT COMMUNITY

appy Valley was once a small, rural and isolated community of farmers. When the town population numbered only in the hundreds, and even when it surpassed one thousand, everyone pretty much knew everyone else like family. If an unfortunate circumstance befell a resident or if someone was in need of help for almost anything, there was always a friendly neighbor who would step up and offer their generosity. If there was one man most willing to offer a helping hand in such a close-knit community, it was lifelong Happy Valley resident Ed Rebstock. Before we understand why Rebstock became affectionately known as "Mr. Happy Valley," we begin with his father, Karl Charles Rebstock.

Charles was born in 1871 in Wurttemberg, Germany, and emigrated in 1888 on the ship *Eider* from Bremen, Germany, to Southampton, England. From there, he continued on to the United States.[217] In 1898, he married Bertha Knauss, and while living in Minnesota, they had their first child, a daughter named Pearl. The Rebstocks then moved to Oregon and settled in Happy Valley, where they had four more children named Esther, Erma, Emery and Edward. In 1901, the Rebstocks were deeded land from John George Zinser, who had purchased the land from John Bennett Deardorff in 1890, and began living in the house Zinser built.[218] Edward "Ed" Alvin Rebstock was born on May 17, 1911, in this home that would later be known as the historic Rebstock house.

As a boy, Ed Rebstock worked on the family farm and attended the East Mount Scott School, a previous name for the schoolhouse in Happy

The Rebstock family (*left to right*): Erma, Pearl, Bertha, Emery, Charles, Esther and Ed. *Happy Valley History Collection.*

Valley.[219] Among the chores he did was to bring in cows from the pasture. In 1930, while working as an unpaid laborer on the family farm, he married Erma Killingbeck. They would have two children together, a son named Karl and a daughter named Barbara.[220] His helping hands were not limited only to the family farm, as his generosity extended to any neighbors in need, which had an effect in the development of the community. He helped build many of Happy Valley's roads and telephone lines. He helped in installing the valley's water system and organizing the Happy Valley Fire District, for which he served as a volunteer for thirty-one years. He helped form the Mount Scott Water District, later renamed Sunrise Water Authority, and served on several boards, including the grade school, his church, the city planning commission and the vigilance committee during the Great Depression.[221] His wife, Erma Rebstock, also worked for the water district, was an active member of the Happy Valley Evangelical Church and managed a three-acre berry patch on their farm.[222]

Other examples of Ed's unhesitant generosity include a time when snow made King Road in front of the school treacherous. Rebstock was there pulling out cars using a team of horses.[223] Rebstock would also herd cattle for neighborhood farmers to the top of Mount Scott, where Willamette

National Cemetery and Lincoln Memorial Park now lie.[224] Longtime Happy Valley resident Noreen Sample wrote about another example of Ed's reliable generosity: "'Call Ed' was the first thought when trouble or catastrophe struck. And Ed always came to the rescue, a kindly knight in friendly guise, quick, efficient, like the day he rescued my basement from ten inches of water when a road culvert was plugged."[225]

In addition to farming his land, Ed Rebstock worked as the superintendent of the Mount Scott Water District for thirty-three years until retiring in 1979.[226] If anything happened with water in the city, Rebstock would come with his tractor and backhoe to fix it.[227] Due to his unselfish endeavors to the point where he knew everyone in the community and everyone knew him, his neighbors affectionately referred to him as "Mr. Happy Valley," a title that he shrugged off but earned despite his humility. Rebstock was so close to his community he even knew the sound of every neighbor's car before seeing it.[228] He was also one of the people who helped start the Happy Valley July 4th fireworks show, now perhaps the biggest day of the year on the Happy Valley city calendar. As a pastime, Ed was an avid outdoorsman who loved going fishing and hunting, with one of his most memorable adventures taking place in Prince Albert, Canada, where he harvested an eight-hundred-pound grizzly bear.[229]

Ed Rebstock at a reservoir site on Mount Scott. *Happy Valley History Collection.*

Rebstock's kindness and view of treating his neighbors like family was shared in the community. Erik Gustafsson, a longtime resident whose family moved to Happy Valley in 1955, described the town as being "very close-knit" while growing up there. "People got along and worked together," he said.[230] This sentiment was also shared by Mike Beutler, son of Happy Valley's first fire chief, William Beutler, who said that while growing up in the valley, the community was a close-knit group where you could drive around and everyone knew who lived where.[231] In 1958, when the volunteer firefighters needed help in the construction of the Happy Valley Fire Station, the community responded to the call in coming together to offer assistance. An early example of the generosity shared by the tightknit community happened in 1904, when a Deardorff Settlement woman identified as "Mrs. Stricke" lost her fence from a careless fire and the valley farmers came together to rebuild it for her. Over a year earlier, the farmers had come together after her husband died and left her a widow; they worked her farm and harrowed her crop free of charge.[232] Another example of the generosity shared among the residents occurred after A.E. Thompson's barn burned down and he lost much of his cattle. The community came together and rebuilt his barn for him. "Everybody knew each other, and when someone was in need, help would come from the community," said Gustafsson.[233]

Ed Rebstock died of cancer on April 12, 1984, after having lived his entire life in the valley. After Ed passed away, the City of Happy Valley purchased the house he was born in and planned a renovation to transform it into the city hall. Unfortunately, due to extensive dry rot and termite damage, the Rebstock house was demolished, and a new building in the style of an old farmhouse, very similar to Ed's home, was built in its place.[234] In 1994, in remembrance of Ed's unselfish service to his neighbors and community, which included using his tractor to help create Happy Valley Park, the city dedicated the Rebstock Park located behind what was then the city hall and later the policing center.[235] Today, you can visit what the author refers to as the "heart of Happy Valley," where King Road and 129th Avenue meet. It is the location of the Happy Valley Policing Center, which sits on the same site of the Rebstock house; Rebstock's workplace, which is now Sunrise Water Authority; the Happy Valley Fire Station, which Rebstock helped organize; and the evangelical church, which Rebstock supported. It is appropriate that this place is the city's "heart," for it was the love of Ed Rebstock for his neighbors that made the close-knit community of Happy Valley such a great place to live.

Chapter 11

FROM ALMOST PORTLAND TO INCORPORATION

Becoming a City

I f you lived in Happy Valley in 1965, you were faced with the possibility that your peaceful, nature-blessed and isolated hollow of barns, horse trails and homes on spacious lots could be swallowed up by annexation into the commercialism of the City of Portland. When Portland annexed the Willamette National Cemetery property and the land on Happy Valley's borders, the valley residents came together to discuss the option of incorporation.[236] When Portland planned to hold a meeting regarding the expansion of the city southward into the hollow, the motivated local residents took immediate action to avoid the prospect of losing their identity as a rural residential community and the fate of paying taxes to the City of Portland. One of those concerned residents was Noreen Sample, who reflected on the situation: "Being grabbed and gobbled up into Multnomah County and Portland was appalling, the desecration of commercialism unthinkable. Happy Valley had to be saved from the fate of losing its individuality."[237]

Community leaders wanted to be the deciding voice in Happy Valley's future, but they would need to hurry. Happy Valley also faced the threat of a new Oregon law that was set to take effect in August that would ban the incorporation of new municipalities within three miles of an existing city.[238] With Happy Valley seated on Portland's border, this new law would apply to them. In June and July, the issue of clarifying Happy Valley's boundaries was settled with the Board of Clackamas County Commissioners. The new city limits were proposed to be set between the Lincoln Memorial Park cemetery and Sunnyside Road. Then, the community held a special election on

Boundary sign along 122nd Avenue in 1988, when Happy Valley city limits were mostly contained within the valley bowl. *Bud Unruh.*

August 25, 1965, to decide whether to incorporate as Clackamas County's eleventh municipality. The community cast their votes at the Happy Valley Fire Station on King Road, and the results ended up favoring incorporation with 111 for and 66 against.[239]

After the people made their voices known, the newly incorporated City of Happy Valley would begin, but without its own basic public services. The fire department would continue to consist of volunteers, and the policing of the city would be provided by the Clackamas County Sheriff's Office.[240] In March 1966, an editorial in the *Oregonian* criticized Happy Valley's incorporation as a city of "convenience" and stated that "taxpayers of the county help subsidize the happiness of Happy Valley."[241] Resident William Beutler, who drove to get the incorporation vote to happen, responded by writing to the paper:

> *The purpose of the incorporation of Happy Valley was not a negative one as you have stated. Our purpose was to preserve a community which is unique in this day and age. Here is a community, that your very editorial page has written in glowing words, where a rural tranquility has been preserved with a minimum of urban services, where neighbors are friends, and the citizen*

continues to have a voice in community affairs and works voluntarily for a way of living that he cherishes. The people of Happy Valley have long been among the first in accepting civic responsibilities. They have risen in this case to protect their community from unnecessary high taxation and encroachment by the City of Portland....The only tax that the people of Happy Valley have avoided is a 25 percent increase that would have resulted from an unwilling annexation into the City of Portland, for which it is doubtful that we would have received a like share of additional services, much less an individual voice in community affairs. [242]

Another reason the residents wanted to incorporate was to prevent commercial development. In 1964, a development group attempted to change zoning in the valley from suburban residential to commercial. Developers sought to build a subdivision with a shopping center and gas station in the center of the valley bowl. After the city incorporated, the citizens approved a city charter and mandated the city council to keep Happy Valley as a rural-residential area without any commercial development. Beutler's wife, Shirley

Happy Valley's first city council. *Standing, left to right:* Alan McEachern, Louis Bauer Jr., James Robnett; *seated:* Jack Kato, Ken Leavens. *City of Happy Valley.*

Beutler, described Happy Valley as a "Shangri-La." "You come over the hill and you're in another world," she said in comparing her city to Portland.[243]

The election for the first city council was held on November 9 with Louis Bauer Jr., Jack Kato, Ken Leavens, Alan McEachern and James Robnett receiving the most votes out of eleven candidates.[244] The newly elected city council held its first meeting on November 17, 1965, at the fire station. Also present at the meeting were Clackamas County commissioner Stan Skoko, city attorney Donald Huffman and acting clerk Robert Bryant. The duties at this initial meeting included electing a mayor and adopting municipal codes to govern the new city. Huffman declared that nominations were open for mayor of the city. Robnett, Kato and Bauer were nominated by their fellow councilmen. The election was held by secret ballot among the councilors, and the ballots were counted by Bryant. The vote ended up as a tie between Robnett and Kato with two votes apiece. It was explained by Commissioner Skoko that the procedure for breaking the draw was by a coin toss. Robnett flipped the coin into the air while Kato called "heads." Robnett won the toss and became the first mayor of Happy Valley.[245] While this is how the event was officially recorded, the actual coin toss happened differently. According to an interview James Robnett gave years later, Jack Kato was actually victorious in the coin toss and won the right to be mayor but chose Robnett to be mayor instead. It was a position Robnett would hold for the next three decades.

Although Happy Valley officially became a city, it would take a long time before it started to look like one. By 1977, after a dozen years as a municipality, Happy Valley had no city taxes. Its $70,000 annual budget was entirely funded by revenue-sharing funds from the county and state. Residents did, however, pay large property taxes because of their landholdings. There was also no city hall, traffic signal, streetlight, restaurant, movie theater, gas station or grocery store. Despite being on Portland's doorstep, it was truly a rural city.[246] A major contributor to keeping Happy Valley a rural city was the leadership of James Robnett, who worked to keep the city's growth at a minimum during his tenure as mayor.

Chapter 12

MAYOR ROBNETT AND STANDING AGAINST URBANIZATION

On November 17, 1965, James Robnett was chosen to be the first mayor of Happy Valley, a position he would be chosen for by city council time and again for the next three decades. Who was this man, and what made him so appealing to the people of the valley? We begin with his early life.

James "Jim" John Robnett was born on August 21, 1926, in Albany, Oregon. By the 1940s, he was living in Pendleton, Oregon, where he graduated from Pendleton High School and was employed by the Pendleton Lumber Company. When the United States entered World War II, he joined the navy.[247] After the war, he graduated from Oregon State University with a degree in mechanical engineering. In 1949, he married Margaret Blackstone on his birthday, and they later had four children together. The Robnett family moved west and eventually settled in Happy Valley in 1958.[248] What attracted James and Margaret to the valley was its rural atmosphere and wanting to give their kids plenty of space to run and have fun growing up.[249]

After Happy Valley incorporated as a municipality in 1965 to preserve its rural way of living and avoid the commercialism of the City of Portland, Robnett wanted to make sure it would stay that way. Following the coin flip with fellow councilman Jack Kato that made him the mayor, Robnett became a leading force to maintain the city as a rural, quiet and residential community. He also possessed a soft-spoken, easygoing personality that allowed him to work well with government officials and his fellow city council members and made him very popular among valley residents.[250]

His popularity stemmed from his willingness to listen to the people and do what was in the best interests of the community. Whenever there was an issue that would affect the city, Mayor Robnett would call for a town meeting and listen to feedback provided by the citizens. Because of his thoughtfulness and caring for other perspectives, he earned respect and admiration from everyone in the city. Although he always looked out for the best interests of maintaining the peace and quiet of Happy Valley's rural way of life, sometimes it would humorously backfire. Such an occurrence happened in the early 1970s, when the city council became tired of motorists speeding through the city. Robnett bought the city's first radar gun to catch the

Mayor James Robnett. *City of Happy Valley.*

speeders. The first perpetrator ended up being the wife of one of the councilors, and this embarrassment led Robnett and the city to not use the radar gun for a while after that.[251]

In addition to being Happy Valley's mayor, Robnett also devoted his time to the Boy Scouts and served as scoutmaster of Troop 191 for ten years. He also enjoyed spending his time fishing, hunting, gardening, fixing cars, reading history books and traveling across Oregon.[252] He was passionate about preserving open areas and green spaces. He helped guide the construction of Happy Valley Park and worked to prevent urbanization as much as he could.[253] While he was mayor, the city successfully prevented a proposal to designate Happy Valley as part of the Portland metro area's Urban Growth Boundary by the Columbia Region Association of Governments (CRAG).[254] The designation would have forced the city to permit development with an increase in property taxes. Mayor Robnett and the city also opposed the Land Conservation and Development Commission (LCDC), which for many years attempted to increase Happy Valley's housing density from 2.4 housing units per acre to 6. Robnett later explained his desire against urbanization: "Once people move here, the feeling is, 'We don't want anybody else here.'"[255] During his time as mayor, the city population grew stagnantly from 1,392 in 1970, to 1,499 in 1980, to 1,519 in 1990. Robnett was determined not to allow the City of Happy Valley to become commercialized. Sandy Coats, who served on the Happy Valley Park Commission in the 1970s prior to becoming the first woman to serve on city council, explained that

City hall along King Road in 1994 during the final year of Robnett's three-decade-long tenure as mayor. *Bud Unruh.*

Mayor Robnett and the city council made a verbal promise to the citizens to not allow any commercial businesses such as restaurants, gas stations or convenience stores in the valley bowl.[256] This was a promise that was kept by city council even after Robnett's tenure as mayor came to an end.

Although Robnett served as Happy Valley's mayor for a long time, it was bound to not last forever. After he was reelected yet again to the city council, the five councilors held the vote to determine council positions in January 1995. James Robnett had always been the choice of the councilmembers to be mayor of the city. But not this time. Newly elected councilman Jim Olsen nominated Randy Nicolay, a councilman first elected in 1992, to be mayor. Votes were cast, and in a surprise result, Robnett was voted out three to one in favor of Nicolay. Olsen nominated Nicolay to become mayor as he felt it was time for a change. He wanted the council to be less involved in the city's daily business and simply make policies and allow the city administrator to carry them out.[257] The leadership change would turn out to be a significant turning point in Happy Valley's history. Not only did the city have a new mayor for the first time in more than twenty-nine years, but there was now no one to stand in the way of urbanization and development. Land developers did acquire some land in the valley during Robnett's final years as mayor, but the growth likely would have been much less significant had he kept his job.

After Robnett retired from city council, Happy Valley quickly turned from pro-rural to pro-urban, a scenario he stood against.

One might wonder why Robnett would volunteer to be mayor for almost three decades. It wasn't to benefit himself financially. Nor did he serve due to a love for the power the position gave him. He considered his job as mayor to be fun and enjoyable thanks to his fellow citizens who also loved him in the job. Time and again, he was reelected to serve on city council. In January 1987, when it was time once again to decide who would serve the next mayoral term, Robnett offered to step aside after twenty-two years and let one of his fellow councilmembers be the city's leader. The councilors all refused, citing their praise for him, and Robnett was selected again by city council to remain mayor.[258] He served tirelessly as Happy Valley's first and, for a long time, only mayor. Another reason he remained mayor for so long was because "I'm the only one dumb enough to keep doing it," he famously quipped. Sharon Fentress, who was the city recorder during many of Robnett's years as mayor, said, "He did what the people wanted. He never did things according to his own agenda."[259] If only every city could be lucky enough to have a mayor like James Robnett. He died on May 10, 2008, and is buried in the Willamette National Cemetery.

Chapter 13

CITY OF TREES

Happy Valley's Parks and Landmarks

B y the early twenty-first century, Happy Valley's massive population and development expansion was well underway. One might have expected its tree cover to vanish in favor of rooftops. This turned out to not be the case, as after Happy Valley made the turn toward urbanization, it was also designated a Tree City, USA. The Arbor Day Foundation's Tree City, USA program offers cities a standard for managing and expanding their public trees. These requirements include a city tree board that is responsible for the care of all trees on city-owned property; a tree ordinance enforced by the city to provide guidance for planting, maintaining and removing trees from public spaces; spending at least two dollars per capita to demonstrate the city's commitment toward trees; and an official annual Arbor Day celebration by the city.[260] When looking over the valley bowl, you can see the city's success as a member of the Tree City, USA program. The city's Comprehensive Plan and Land Development Code preserved green spaces and natural areas by limiting development within areas of natural resources and steep slopes. These efforts preserved Happy Valley as a beautiful city to live in. When we go into the trees, we can explore the city's many great parks and landmarks.

Happy Valley's first city park, the aptly named Happy Valley Park, began when Robert Francis and his wife, Doris, decided to sell their farm. William Beutler, Happy Valley's fire chief, heard of their plans and inquired of his valley neighbors whether their property could be purchased and made into a park. In 1962, eight Happy Valley homeowners donated money to purchase

Happy Valley Park as it appeared in 1992. *Happy Valley History Collection.*

twenty acres to help make the park dream a reality. The first portion of land was purchased in 1963 and the other in 1964. The locals responsible for the land purchase were called the Mount Scott Investment Group, and they included Neil Reigleman, Bill Jinnings, Lew Smith, Ken Leavens, Bill Dietz, Don Krause, Jack Allen and Omar Throndsen. As Happy Valley was not yet an incorporated city, Clackamas County accepted the property as a county park. After Happy Valley incorporated, the city planned to use Oregon gas tax money to make improvements to the park. The city persuaded Clackamas County to deed the park to the City of Happy Valley, as they had no funds available to make improvements to the park. The city then appointed a commission to supervise improvements. A dinner and auction were held at Happy Valley Elementary School to raise funds for the first park improvements. In 1966, Mayor James Robnett led a group of volunteers to plow, level and build a Little League baseball field. Various volunteer groups helped over the years in improving the park, including the Boy Scouts, Girl Scouts, 4-H, Little Leaguers, Park Commission members and city citizens.[261] In the 1970s, the park's paved road was constructed and the tennis courts and a playground were installed.[262] There were also horse riding paths through the park for exercise. Barbara Smith was the city's park commission chairwoman and provided a history of the park for the city's twentieth anniversary in 1985.[263] The skate park at Happy Valley Park officially opened in 2013. The process began in 1999 when grade schooler Armani Lopez Guererro proposed his idea for a skate park to the Happy Valley Parks Advisory Committee. Years later, his younger brother Christopher Lopez Hale gathered signatures and presented the idea to the committee. After meeting with contractors, the parks committee proposed building the skate park to city council, and it approved.[264] The All Abilities Park, designed to promote the healthy development of all children's physical, cognitive and sensory abilities, opened at Happy Valley Park in October 2019.[265] The park's gazebo has become known as "the city's living room."[266]

To the east of the Happy Valley Park is one of the city's notable landmarks: Scouters Mountain. This mountain is more of a hill or knoll and reaches about seven hundred feet above sea level. The slopes have not always been covered in trees. The Douglas firs on the lower elevated northern half were logged off in the early 1950s. After Corey Gustafsson, who later served on the city planning commission for many years, and his family moved to Happy Valley in late 1955, they soon found the open slope covered in snow. Being of Norwegian ancestry, they were a skiing family and took advantage of the winter storm by skiing down the cleared hillside of Scouters Mountain.[267] Before being known by that name, the hill was known by some residents as "Guidi's Hill." This name came from local farmers Abraham and Edith Guidi. Edith was born in 1887 to John Bennett Deardorff, Christian Deardorff's grandson. Her husband, Abraham "Abe" Guidi, was originally from Italy and came to the United States in about 1899.[268] Abe and Edith's farm was located along 145th Avenue near King Road and up the slope of Scouters Mountain.[269] The name Scouters Mountain originated from a Boy Scouts camp that was located there.

Scouters Mountain was home to Camp Discovery, which was used for Scout training and camping. Camp Discovery consisted of approximately 190 acres of land.[270] Portland-area members of the Boy Scouts of America started building a training center lodge there in 1955. It opened in 1956 and was formally dedicated on May 11, 1957. The flagpoles at the lodge were dedicated to the Scouts who served and lost their lives in World War II.[271] The two-story, seventeen-thousand-square-foot lodge was built in a rustic style similar to Timberline Lodge on Mount Hood in a grove of fir trees. The Scouts' main purpose for the lodge was as a place for adult volunteers to become scoutmasters.[272] The property included the lodge, barns, a radio

The architect's preliminary sketch for the Chief Obie Lodge in 1954. *Jim Hill, Cascade Pacific Council, BSA.*

building and camping areas.[273] The lodge was named for George Herman Oberteuffer, who was chief executive of the Boy Scouts of America in the Portland area for thirty-two years from 1925 until his retirement in 1957. His nickname was "Obie." He was born in Washington, D.C., but grew up in Portland, Oregon.[274] Oberteuffer was known as the "granddaddy of Oregon scouting" and founded numerous Boy Scout camps, including the training center on Scouters Mountain. After his death, the Columbia Pacific Council of the Boy Scouts of America, which later changed its name to the Cascade Pacific Council, honored him by naming the lodge Chief Obie Lodge. His memorial service was held at the lodge, and attendees included his son-in-law Senator Bob Packwood and Oregon governor Vic Atiyeh.[275]

Chief Obie Lodge could accommodate about three hundred people, and the Boy Scouts opened it to the public for various events. The lodge hosted weddings and receptions, churches held retreats and Easter Sunday services there and even groups from England stayed there.[276] The Girl Scouts also assembled at the Scouters Mountain training center.[277] Although the Boy Scouts camp was popular, it did face conflict. Henry Troh, a Portland flight instructor, was the owner of an airstrip by 162nd Avenue on the eastern side of Scouters Mountain. Troh bought his original land for the airstrip in 1957. The Scouts then purchased a three-acre site to prevent him from expanding his airfield to preserve the natural area near the training center and to prevent planes from flying over the lodge. Troh owned the land around the three-acre site and offered to purchase it from the Scouts to build an alternate landing strip. The Scouts refused, which resulted in a dispute between them

The Chief Obie Lodge under construction on Scouters Mountain. *Jim Hill, Cascade Pacific Council, BSA.*

and Troh. The Scouts offered to sell Troh the three acres if he agreed to a clause that planes would follow an eastwardly traffic pattern. Henry Troh also refused.[278] Troh developed his own airfield and flight school in Portland and was a flight instructor for Tex Rankin in California. He taught thousands of students until he sold his Portland airport and moved to 162nd Avenue by Scouters Mountain to build a private airfield called Troh's Nest.[279] He died in 1968 and was buried at Lincoln Memorial Park on Mount Scott.

One of Happy Valley's darkest events occurred at the lodge. On January 15, 1987, forty-eight-year-old Jimmy Nails was murdered by his seventeen-year-old son at the Scouters Mountain lodge. The younger Nails shot his sleeping father twice in the head with a rifle and then fled in his father's car to California to see his ex-girlfriend. The father and son had lived together at the lodge, where Jimmy was the custodian. His body was discovered in the evening by the camp ranger, Vernon Christy.[280] The son was arrested the night of January 15 in California. The younger Nails claimed he became depressed following a breakup with his girlfriend, who moved to California and took cocaine and methamphetamine. While high on drugs, he took a rifle out of the gun cabinet and killed his father.[281] The son was found guilty of manslaughter, not murder, due to the judge deciding he was under "an extreme emotional disturbance" at the time of the crime, and was sentenced to twenty years in prison. Jimmy Nails was remembered fondly by many of the Boy Scouts who stayed at the camp, as he always made sure they had whatever they needed to enjoy their time there.[282]

The Chief Obie Lodge served thousands of guests annually until 2004. That year, the state fire marshal closed the lodge following complaints about fire danger from the lodge's lack of sprinklers. The Scouts had ceased overnight stays at the lodge, but despite warnings from the fire marshal, they were unable to get funds to install the required sprinklers.[283] In 2010, the Cascade Pacific Council reached a deal with Metro to sell a portion of their property for them to turn it into a nature park.[284] In 2011, the Chief Obie Lodge was demolished. The deconstruction was devastating to many people involved in the Scouts, including Dave Bair, who was the last ranger of the lodge. When Bair's father brought him there as a kid in the 1970s, he fell in love with the lodge and the area.[285] Following the deconstruction, the property that was owned by the Boy Scouts was turned into a park by Metro, and Scouters Mountain Nature Park opened on August 28, 2014.[286]

Another of Happy Valley's notable landmarks is Mount Scott, the city's highest point that rises to more than one thousand feet above sea level. Although Scott features more homes than the city's other high points at Scouters Mountain and Mount Talbert, there are still many trees on the butte. Much of the old timber on this mountain was burned by a forest fire during Happy Valley's pioneer farming days and replaced by virgin timber.[287] The butte's namesake comes from *Oregonian* newspaper editor Harvey Scott. In 1889, William P. Keady, who was a printer and publisher, was looking at purchasing the property of A.C. Fairchild, which at the time was called Mount Zion. Keady agreed to purchase the property but needed a partner to pay half of the amount. Keady asked Harvey Scott if he knew of any interested persons to partner with him. Scott decided to go with Keady to look at the property and agreed to partner with Keady himself. Without Scott's knowledge, Keady went to local map makers and asked them to change the name of Mount Zion to Mount Scott, possibly to show gratitude for Mr. Scott's financial partnership. Harvey Scott later purchased hundreds of adjoining acres and Keady's portion of the original property.[288]

On Mount Scott, bordering Happy Valley, is the Lincoln Memorial Park cemetery. Prior to that name, it was known as the Mount Scott Park Cemetery, and articles of incorporation for the Mount Scott Cemetery Corporation were filed in 1909.[289] The Mount Scott Park Cemetery was formally dedicated on May 30, 1912, with an estimated six thousand people in attendance.[290] In 1926, the cemetery officially changed its name to Lincoln Memorial Park in honor of President Abraham Lincoln.[291] On the opposite side of Mount Scott Boulevard, the Willamette National Cemetery opened as a resting place for armed forces service members and their spouses. In February 1951, Blaine Clayton Van Ausdeln, a World War I veteran, became the first person to be buried in the Willamette National Cemetery.[292]

Back in the valley bowl, a smaller park was created in 1994 behind what was then the city hall, later remodeled as the policing center, on King Road called Rebstock Park. The City of Happy Valley dedicated this new park in remembrance of Ed Rebstock for his generosity and service to his neighbors and support of the community.[293] By Sunnyside Road, the third of Happy Valley's major landmarks, Mount Talbert, reaches an elevation of 740 feet. Once known as Mount Latourette, from the prominent Oregon City family who once owned property on the butte, it was later named Talbert's Hill, likely for Daniel Talbert, who owned a homestead on the western slope and for his family members in lived in the Happy Valley and Clackamas areas. The forested hill is home to Mount Talbert Nature Park, which Metro held a grand opening for on October 6, 2007.[294] Visitors can enjoy a hike across more than four miles of trails through tall firs and white oaks while on the lookout for birds of many varieties. A major park that opened south of Sunnyside Road just east of 152nd Avenue is the Hidden Falls Nature Park. Prior to receiving this name, the waterfall was known as Rock Creek Falls, named for Rock Creek, which cascades over the 22-foot drop on its way to converging with the Clackamas River. In the early twentieth century, locals from the Sunnyside and Rock Creek communities would swim and fish at the falls.[295] After the area was privately owned for decades, the North Clackamas Parks and Recreation District announced in 2017 that it was acquiring more than twenty-one acres of wooded area around the falls site that had been inaccessible to the public to create a new park. The parks district partnered with Icon Construction to develop what was named the Hidden Falls Nature Park, which included a paved trail, bridge and viewing and picnic area overlooking the falls. The park opened on June 22, 2019.[296]

In 2006, Happy Valley citizens voted to join the North Clackamas Parks and Recreation District. At the time, the top four projects proposed to be built in Happy Valley were a Rock Creek community park, a recreation center, an all-weather soccer field and to extend the Mount Scott Trail to Mount Talbert.[297] City and Clackamas County officials signed a contract

The waterfall along Rock Creek at Hidden Falls Nature Park. *Happy Valley History Collection.*

that transferred development fees from the City of Happy Valley to the North Clackamas district for park projects in the city. North Clackamas Parks and Recreation built the Hood View Park in Happy Valley in 2009. As the years went by, city officials became increasingly dissatisfied with the lack of park developments and completed projects in the city. Then, in 2017, the North Clackamas district announced plans to sell the only park they built in the city to the North Clackamas School District in exchange for more than $15 million and properties in Milwaukie and Oak Grove. Happy Valley city officials viewed this as the parks district taking funds from the city and using them elsewhere, and in 2017, the city council voted to withdraw from North Clackamas Parks and Recreation to form their own district.[298]

The city council's vote to withdraw Happy Valley from the district led to a dispute with Clackamas County, which oversaw the North Clackamas district. In May 2018, more than 70 percent of Happy Valley residents approved a levy to fund maintenance and operations for Happy Valley Parks and Recreation.[299] In March, prior to the levy, the Oregon Department of Revenue approved Happy Valley's request to withdraw from North Clackamas Parks. In June, after the levy passed, the Department of Revenue rescinded the approval due to a technical error in that the request had not been submitted by the proper authority—the Clackamas County Board of Commissioners. This meant that Happy Valley taxpayers could legally be subjected by both Clackamas County and Happy Valley to fund both parks and recreation districts. Mayor Lori Chavez-DeRemer vowed not to double tax her citizens.[300] In September 2018, the Oregon Tax Court ruled in favor of the city and ordered the Department of Revenue to approve the withdrawal. In response to the decision, the county filed a lawsuit against the city in circuit court, arguing the city did not use the appropriate statute to withdraw from North Clackamas Parks.[301] In August 2019, a Clackamas County Circuit Court jury awarded the return of more than $18 million to the City of Happy Valley from a breach of contract by North Clackamas Parks, as they determined that the park projects planned to be built by the North Clackamas district had not been delivered.[302]

In December 2019, Happy Valley and Clackamas County officials reached an agreement to finally settle the dispute. State Representatives Janelle Bynam and Mark Meek helped end the dispute by supporting legislation to allow Happy Valley to withdraw from the North Clackamas district. The city agreed to accept a smaller payment than what the jury awarded to move forward with withdrawal and avoid years of litigation.[303] In the city and county's agreement, they jointly supported state legislation to allow Happy Valley to withdraw and create their own parks and recreation district. The county also agreed to pay more than $14 million to the City of Happy Valley and transfer park property from North Clackamas Parks to the city that included property by Mount Talbert, Hidden Falls Nature Park, Mount Scott Creek Trail and other sites.[304] Finally, in July 2020, the Happy Valley Parks and Recreation District opened its first season of programming. With the City of Happy Valley now in control of its parks and related programming, they can decide if this city of trees will expand its parks potential into the future.

Chapter 14

WALLY'S WORLD

Remembering Sunnyside's Popular Swimming Hole

T he Sunnyside community, an area that became identified with Happy Valley, was once home to a special oasis. On private property surrounded by cedar woods was a popular swimming hole in a parklike setting that was a must-see destination for thousands of locals and a heaven on earth for one soft-spoken and generous man. His name was Wallace Melvin Hubbard, but he was better known as "Wally." This is his story and way of remembering the world he created.

Wally Hubbard was born on July 29, 1922, the seventh of twelve children born to Alma and Walter Hubbard.[305] Walter was a farmer and a lifelong resident of Sunnyside, while Alma Kunze, her maiden name, was born in Germany.[306] The Hubbards owned property along what is now 132nd Avenue, midway between Sunnyside Road and Highway 212.[307] This road south of Sunnyside Road became known as Hubbard Lane before the name changed to 132nd Avenue. The land was all timber before there were houses and farms. On their farm, the Hubbards raised berries and cucumbers and had cows, horses and chickens on several acres. Everyone in the family worked on the farm, and that was their livelihood. It was the job of the children to trample down the hay, and Wally enjoyed jumping down from the beam inside the barn into the hay.[308] As a teenager, Wally worked as an unpaid laborer on the family farm. He attended the small Sunnyside School that became Sunnyside Community Church, where he would be an active member, and attended Milwaukie High School, where he was a freshman in the 1936–37 school year but did not appear in subsequent yearbooks. He

Swimmers at Wally Hubbard's dam in the 1970s. *Verna Ashton.*

was drafted into the army during World War II and served in the Medical Corps in New Caledonia in the south Pacific and Okinawa, Japan.[309]

In 1946, a natural occurrence would impact Wally's life. A giant tree fell across Sieben Creek and created a spontaneous dam on his property between 132nd and 142nd Avenues. Rather than remove the fallen timber, the new pond gave Wally an idea—to turn the impeded creek into a swimming hole for local kids.[310] At first, Wally Hubbard created a wooden dam. But before he pursued the swimming hole further, Hubbard decided to reenlist in the army because he felt called by God to do so. After he returned home in 1949, Wally refocused on the dam. With the help of his brothers, they built a concrete dam nine feet high and eighty feet wide with an outlet in the middle that could be closed with wooden planks.[311] After Wally's swimming hole came to fruition, he reenlisted again—his third stint in the army—during the Korean War. After a few more years of service to his country, he returned to his seven-and-a-half-acre world to live one mile from the farmhouse where he grew up.[312] Wally then transitioned from serving his country to serving his community. He worked mainly as a substitute mail carrier for the U.S. Postal Service, using his own car to deliver mail throughout Clackamas and Damascus. He did other odd jobs until 1981, when he retired.[313] When he wasn't working or maintaining the dam, Wally loved climbing Mount Hood, ascending

Oregon's highest point about forty-eight times in his life. As a Christian, he felt the mountain brought him closer to God. One of Wally's climbs almost became a disaster in 1976. While leading a climbing party of five, they slid eighty feet into a crevasse while descending the Hogsback on the upper slopes of Mount Hood. They survived with only cuts and bruises.[314]

As the years went by, word spread about Wally's dam, and the swimming hole became very popular. He offered the pond for free, with admission being granted if visitors attended church or Sunday school at least twice a month. There was also no cussing, no smoking and no drinking allowed.[315] Wally built a rope swing, a merry-go-round, monkey bars, a Tarzan rope that spanned the width of the pond, a boathouse and later a waterslide up the steep slope on the northeast end of the pond.[316] Church groups, families and picnickers journeyed there during the summer to enjoy the eight-foot-deep water and its shady cedar surroundings. Churches also held special services and baptisms there, and Wally's creation became a local attraction.[317] Linda Zinser Negus recalled that after berry picking in Happy Valley, she and her family went to Wally's dam to wash their berries. She described it as a fun place to go growing up and a highlight of her childhood.[318] In 1966, Wally and some family members constructed a 60-foot-long water slide, 25 feet high, made of wood, lined with fiberglass and kept slippery with running water. The new addition made the swimming hole even more popular. Children would ride their bikes from as far as Gresham to swim in Wally's swimming hole. Hubbard provided a picnic table, wooden rafts and rubber inner tubes for kids to play with in the water. If Wally wasn't around keeping watch, he hired a lifeguard. He extended the slide several times until 1971, when it reached a heart-pounding 340 feet long. The kids weren't free to do whatever they wanted. If any misbehaved, Hubbard banished them. Thousands of visitors enjoyed the dam over the years; sometimes hundreds would come in a single day, crowding the streets of 142nd Avenue and Charjan Street with parked vehicles.[319]

Wally Hubbard's generosity in sharing his private park with thousands of people was not without controversy. Injuries would sometimes occur, which Hubbard blamed on the careless exuberance of some young swimmers. County Sanitarian John Borden considered the water too dangerous to swim in because of its murkiness. Sunnyside–Happy Valley fire chief Milt Durham voiced his concerns after watching injuries occur at the slide, calling the water "dangerously opaque" and the slide "hazardous." The most serious accident happened in 1969, when eighteen year-old Dean Mayer of Oregon City died of pneumonia in a Portland hospital after he fell from the slide

The thrilling waterslide at Wally's dam in the 1970s. *Verna Ashton*.

and nearly drowned.[320] The tragedy did not land Wally in any known legal trouble, nor did it deter him from extending the slide even farther. In 1971, when the slide reached 340 feet, Clackamas County charged Hubbard with building an unsafe structure according to their building codes. A trial date was set for October in the County Circuit Court. Hubbard's lawyer filed a response denying the slide was unsafe.[321] But in September, Hubbard relented and allowed Clackamas County building inspector Charles Bartl, who had deemed the slide structurally unsafe, to direct a group of volunteers from the Clackamas County Homebuilders Association to remove 140 feet from the slide and reinforce it. The effort saved Wally from legal troubles, and tests on the suspected unsanitary water proved otherwise.[322] The swimming hole remained popular until 1991, when heavy rains washed tons of dirt, loosened by upstream housing construction, into the creek that filled the dam. The water silted up; the slide, rope swing and rafts went away; and Wally's park lost its popularity.[323]

Hubbard's generosity extended beyond the dam. He was an active member of Sunnyside Community Church and several senior citizen groups.[324] Rather than living comfortably, Wally gave away much of his pension and Social Security money to support poor families living in India,

Indonesia, Haiti, the Dominican Republic, Ecuador and the Philippines and to aid pastors and missionaries. He kept only enough money to eat and to drive around in an old car. He had no insurance or savings. After his house burned to the ground in the 1980s, rather than rebuild or move, he lived simply in a small camping trailer.[325] Serving others was more important to Wally Hubbard than serving himself. Of the dam, he said, "I built it for God-fearing, God-loving people." Being close to God was important to Wally. One of his signs leading to the pond read, "The fear of the Lord is the beginning of knowledge, but fools despise wisdom and discipline."[326]

Perhaps Hubbard got wise about the fun but dangerous slide and conceded that it needed to be cut back. Eventually, it was removed altogether. Was he arrogant or ignorant when it came to the slide's danger? In those days, there was no North Clackamas Aquatic Park for kids to safely swim in and have fun. The closest accessible alternative for a place to swim was the Clackamas River, which would have been far more dangerous than Wally's dam. Who knows? Maybe he saved the lives of many youngsters by creating his swimming hole. The world Wally created made him into a beloved figure

The site of Wally's dam as it appeared in 2020. *Happy Valley History Collection.*

beyond his Sunnyside neighborhood. He just loved the kids and watching them have fun. As he was a lifelong bachelor and had no children of his own, this probably further inspired him to want to bring joy and share his seven-and-a-half-acre plot of land with his neighbors and their children. He dedicated his life to serving others—his country, his community, total strangers living on the other side of the world and God. He wasn't perfect, but our world could be a little better if we were a little more like Wally Hubbard. Hubbard died on January 29, 2008, and was buried in the Willamette National Cemetery.

Chapter 15

CLACKAMAS TOWN CENTER
AND FORESHADOWING
HAPPY VALLEY'S FATE

J ust west of Interstate 205 is a place that has more history to it than it might seem. It was once an undeveloped field that became an economic and commercial hub for the north Clackamas County region that includes the City of Happy Valley. It is a premier shopping destination in the Portland metro area that is more than just a shopping mall. The story of the Clackamas Town Center would foreshadow the fate of another area of rural farmland that it would later become identified with—Happy Valley.

Clackamas Town Center got its start from the vision of Ernest W. Hahn, a Southern California developer and shopping center magnate. Hahn had succeeded and failed to build other major shopping malls in California, Washington and New Mexico as he faced legal challenges from residents and environmentalists.[327] In the early 1970s, he set his sights on undeveloped land in a small residential area of unincorporated Clackamas County between Milwaukie and Happy Valley. It was a field of cows, radio towers, blackberry bushes and scrub brush, and on the south side of Sunnyside Road were residential houses.[328] The land he envisioned for a mall was owned by the North Clackamas School District. The site was designated for a fourth high school after Milwaukie, Clackamas and Rex Putnam. But after voters rejected proposals by the school district to finance construction of another high school, the school board elected to sell the property in 1973 for $805,000 to Coldwell Banker, whose chairman, Hahn, planned to build a shopping center. Surrounding acreage would also be purchased for the project. The school district also rejected a competing bid from Fred Meyer.[329]

Completion was originally set for 1976, but construction of the Town Center faced several delays due to regulatory requirements, challenges to zoning approval and protests.[330] Clackamas Town Center's comprehensive plan was proposed by Hahn's California-based development firm. The proposal was supported by the County Planning Commission, Milwaukie City Council, North Clackamas Chamber of Commerce and the North Clackamas Citizens Committee. They believed the center would provide jobs, tax benefits and convenient shopping; promote orderly development; and discourage strip commercial growth in the area. Opponents of the plan included the South of Sunnyside Neighborhood League, Tri-County New Politics and the Oregon Environmental Council. The South of Sunnyside Neighborhood League was a group of residents who opposed the Town Center development. They argued the mall would increase noise, traffic and pollution and add to economic problems for existing shopping stores.[331] The North Clackamas School District Board supported the proposed Town Center because it believed the mall would have a positive impact on the characteristics of the 82nd Avenue corridor and the Interstate 205 area and would generate additional tax revenues. A poll of Happy Valley residents, who notably enjoyed living in a rural, residential-only setting, narrowly supported the project, 118 in favor to 102 opposed.[332]

A comprehensive plan to allow development of the Town Center was approved by the Clackamas County Board of Commissioners in 1975 in a two-to-one decision. Commissioner Stan Skoko approved the Town Center request on the basis that it would discourage strip zoning development, improve transit, provide job opportunities to North Clackamas County residents and boost economic benefits to the county. Board chairman Tom Telford agreed with Skoko to approve the Town Center request. Commissioner Robert Schumacher voted against it, as he was concerned with the overall impact on people living about half a mile away from the site.[333] Development for the site received approval from the Oregon Department of Environmental Quality (DEQ) in 1976 and authorized 6,500 parking spaces to be created. The DEQ listed a number of requirements for its approval, including provisions for mass transit, bus shelters and widening and improving the roads surrounding the site.[334] While Hahn's development firm was getting the necessary approvals, the South of Sunnyside Neighborhood League won a legal battle with the Oregon Supreme Court ruling that the Town Center didn't conform to Clackamas County's comprehensive land-use plan. The county then revised its plan and rezoned the site and the neighborhood for commercial

The food court at Clackamas Town Center shortly after the mall opened in 1981. *Clackamas County Historical Society.*

development. Soon the Sunnyside Road residents moved away, and the Clackamas Promenade, across from the Town Center, was built.[335]

County planners hoped the Hahn project would serve a role beyond just a shopping mall. They hoped the site would become the center of a highly developed urban community.[336] After all its legal delays, Clackamas Town Center finally opened on March 6, 1981. Architect John Graham and Company of Seattle designed the $125 million shopping mall, and it opened

The towering wood-sculpted cedar trees in the center court at Clackamas Town Center in about 2003. *Clackamas County Historical Society.*

with one million square feet of retail space, making it one of the largest shopping centers in Oregon. The first five anchor stores were JCPenney, Meier & Frank, Nordstrom, Sears and Montgomery Ward.[337] Among its unique features were a Clackamas County branch library, a five-screen theater, three towering wood-sculpted cedar trees, community meeting rooms and an Olympic-sized ice-skating rink.[338]

Since the mall's opening, it has seen several new beginnings through remodels. The library, which was located in a nook near the ice rink, closed in 1996 and relocated northeast of the Town Center.[339] The ice rink received national attention when Tonya Harding practiced there during her career and when it was remodeled as the Dorothy Hamill Skating Centre in 1994. The famous ice rink, which provided the perfect entertainment for visitors dining in the surrounding food court, closed in 2003 due to operational expenses and competition from other rinks.[340] The three cedar sculptures, each more than thirty feet in height, were removed in 2004 as part of a $100 million makeover of the mall.[341] On September 12, 2009, the Town Center provided a vital link in transportation when the first MAX Light Rail Line to extend into Clackamas County, the Green Line, opened.[342] With the 2001 bankruptcy of Montgomery Ward, the 2018 closure of Sears, the 2020 closure of Nordstrom and Meier & Frank being replaced by Macy's, the JCPenney store became the last remaining member of the original anchor stores.

Clackamas Town Center received national attention in 2012, when a shooting rampage took the lives of Cindy Ann Yuille and Steven Forsyth.[343] The Town Center sign along Sunnyside Road became a memorial to the victims of the tragedy. The Town Center fell on difficult times, as did many businesses, when it was forced to close in March 2020 due to the outbreak of the COVID-19 pandemic. The mall began gradual reopening in late May. In 2021, the Town Center's parking garage hosted a drive-through clinic to administer COVID-19 vaccinations. In September 2020, when wildfires raged across Clackamas County and evacuations were ordered, displaced residents from Oregon City to Estacada flocked to Clackamas Town Center in their trailers and RVs, which made the parking lot look like a campground. In response, the Clackamas Rotary, Stanford's Restaurant, local church groups and other generous persons provided free food to the evacuees.[344]

Clackamas Town Center was once located in an undeveloped, rural and residential area. Then development proponents and pro-growth visionaries brought forth change that transformed the once quiet area into an economic and commercial hub. Despite all the changes, Clackamas Town Center has maintained its reputation from the beginning as being more than just a shopping mall. It's a vital part of the region for the economy and a community center for local residents. Although Happy Valley residents did not know it when they narrowly supported the Town Center idea in the 1970s, the mall development and changes foreshadowed what would happen to small, quiet, rural Happy Valley by the end of the twentieth century.

Chapter 16

PRO-GROWTH TAKES OVER

Becoming Oregon's Fastest-Growing City

etween 1990 and 2020, the City of Happy Valley was the fastest-growing city in Oregon by population percentage increase. Until the 1990s, Happy Valley's population growth was minimal. The first three censuses of the city counted 1,392 residents in 1970, 1,499 in 1980 and 1,519 in 1990. The 2020 U.S. census counted Happy Valley's population as 23,733 for an increase of more than 1,462 percent since 1990. Sherwood, the second-fastest-growing city in Oregon over the same period, grew from 3,093 in 1990 to 20,450 in 2020 for an increase of 561 percent. How did Happy Valley become Oregon's fastest-growing city in terms of population percentage growth since the 1990s? First, we must understand why the city's growth failed to occur over a longer period of time.

Happy Valley incorporated as a municipality in 1965 to prevent a fate of being annexed into the city of Portland and to protect its identity as a small, rural community of pastures sprinkled with houses. But the fight to protect that precious identity was not over. In 1977, most Happy Valley residents opposed a proposal to designate their city as part of the Portland metro area's Urban Growth Boundary.[345] The designation would have forced the city to permit development with an increase in property taxes. In 1978, the Metropolitan Service District included Happy Valley within Portland's Urban Growth Boundary, and the decision led to a fight over housing density.[346] In 1980, the city adopted its first Comprehensive Plan with a housing density of 2.4 units per acre.[347] However, that contrasted with the Land Conservation and Development Commission (LCDC) that Happy Valley's housing density should be 6 units per acre. Eventually, the city ran out of money in its fight against the LCDC in court. The dispute between the city and the commission lasted until 1985, when the two sides reached a compromise to increase the housing density to 6 houses per acre while including protections for the city's spacious environment.[348]

Another hurdle to clear before the city could grow was the lack of a sewer system. The LCDC required developable areas to provide such services. A 1987 Happy Valley City Council survey of 331 residents resulted in 72 percent favoring the continued use of private septic tanks over a proposed citywide sewer system.[349] Michael Hurlburt, my father, who moved to Happy Valley in 1970, explained that developers couldn't build because water would drain out onto somebody else's property and that residents didn't want to change over to the sewer pipes unless their septic tanks failed because of the costs to do so. However, public sanitary systems would be extended into the Happy Valley area, and city growth was made possible by these extensions and others.[350] Development would remain lethargic until the 1990s, when there was a change in city leadership.

From 1965 to 1994, Mayor James Robnett worked to delay urbanization of the valley for as long as possible. His tenure ended abruptly in January 1995 when the city council, featuring newly elected members who wanted to see change, surprisingly elected Councilor Randy Nicolay as mayor.[351] Had Robnett kept his job, a notable population increase still would have occurred due to new subdivisions built on land acquired by developers during his final mayoral years.[352] However, the growth likely would have been much less significant. Sharon Fentress, who was the city recorder during many of James Robnett's years as mayor, recalled that after he was ousted as the city's leader, Happy Valley became a totally different city.[353] Bill Brandon, who worked as Happy Valley's city administrator, remarked in 1995 about the town's growth potential while overlooking the valley: "You're going to look down over this, and it's going to be rooftops instead of trees....That's kind of hard for people to believe, that they're going to have to give it up."[354] The shift in city power gave development proponents more influence over the city's growth potential and proved to be a turning point, as there was now no one to stand in the way of urbanization from taking over the city. Eugene Grant, who became mayor in 1999, favored development and annexation but also understood why Happy Valley citizens desired maintaining the status quo. He believed the city needed to manage, not try to prevent, growth and change.[355] In an interview in 2002, Mayor Grant said, "If the city's got to grow, in some ways it's easier to get it done all at once. The sooner you can get the growth finished, the sooner you can mature as a city."[356]

Happy Valley's population boom would be aided by the city expanding beyond the valley bowl between Mount Scott and Scouters Mountain. With the city council led by Mayor Robnett promising that there would be no retail businesses in the valley, this led to the city expanding into the Sunnyside area to build retail businesses out there. In the 1980s, when the city limits had not reached beyond the bowl, Happy Valley had 1,450 acres of land.[357] By 2006, the city was 4,524 acres in size. By 2020, the city had grown to more than 7,400 acres.[358] As the city's total area has added existing populated land or developable property, it has seen concurrent population growth. In 2000, Happy Valley voters approved annexing 582 acres in the Rock Creek area into the city, increasing the size of the City of Happy Valley by about 33 percent in just one move.[359] The city then adopted the Rock Creek Comprehensive Plan in 2001 to envision a transformation of the area with family residences, retail establishments and office buildings.[360] In 2002, Happy Valley voters approved a measure that gave the city council authority in the next five years to approve annexations east of the city without gaining voter approval for each annexation request.[361] One of the major annexations the city council passed unanimously was in 2004 to add 891 acres from 147th

Looking west at a pumpkin patch from 152nd Avenue south of Sunnyside Road in 1989. *Bud Unruh.*

The pumpkin patch site at 152nd Avenue in 2014 showing the effects of pro-growth development in the Happy Valley area. *Bud Unruh.*

Avenue eastward to 177th Avenue, which was an informal boundary line set by Damascus town leaders. This annexation included Scouters Mountain, which had not been within Happy Valley's city limits to that point.[362] In 2016, the Happy Valley City Council voted four to one to approve building about six hundred houses on the east side of Scouters Mountain. The lone vote against the proposal was councilor and future mayor Tom Ellis. Happy Valley citizens voiced their opposition to the housing development in that it would block a natural wildlife corridor and increase traffic in an already highly congested area along 145th and 147th Avenues down to Sunnyside Road.[363] Out of the belief the housing project would have a harshly negative impact on the environment, wildlife and nearby homeowners, a group of citizens attempted to block the development, but their efforts were unsuccessful.[364] The area was clear-cut, and development commenced. People who lived in unincorporated areas have also moved to Happy Valley by voluntarily annexing their properties into the city. Former Oregon state representative Patrick Sheehan decided to annex his property into the city limits, as he found it would be easier to obtain a permit to add an extension onto his house as a Happy Valley resident.[365]

Despite the population boom, Happy Valley has maintained green spaces and livability thanks to regulations on development. In 2017, Steve Koper, Happy Valley's planning services manager at the time, explained that the city's Comprehensive Plan and Land Development Code preserves green spaces and natural areas by protecting and limiting development within areas

The land on the southeast side of Scouters Mountain while being cleared for a housing development in 2017. *Happy Valley History Collection.*

The subdivision at Scouters Mountain in 2023. *Happy Valley History Collection.*

of natural resources and steep slopes.[366] When overlooking the valley bowl, one can see the city's success as a member of the Tree City, USA program. Happy Valley's steep slope ordinance has also prevented subdivisions from being constructed on the slopes of Scouters Mountain. Tree canopy and wildlife habitat persevere. Deer are occasionally seen crossing roads in the city. These all contribute to Happy Valley's uniqueness as a city, which can help explain why so many people want to live here.

Lastly, Happy Valley has seen its population rise due to a good reputation in the Portland area as a great place to live. In 2002, Mayor Eugene Grant said that a significant part of the city's growth was due to its reputation as a great place to raise children.[367] Grant himself moved to Happy Valley for his children to attend the local schools in the North Clackamas School District. Happy Valley's schools have all been built or at least seen significant modern remodeling in the twenty-first century. Happy Valley's convenient access to Interstate 205, the Clackamas River and Mount Hood territories and employment opportunities in the Portland area also add to its reputation as a desirable place to live. The city has also worked hard to maintain Happy Valley's "smaller community" feeling through programs, events and the city's neighborly residents. The fact that Happy Valley focuses more on feeling like a community than a city makes it a special place. Along with the land-use laws, sewer system, pro-growth officials, annexations and good reputation help explain how Happy Valley became Oregon's fastest-growing city. Happy Valley has seen explosive growth since the 1990s, but not at the cost of its quality of livability.

Chapter 17

A SMALL TOWN NO MORE

The City of Happy Valley was once a small, quiet, rural town of farms sequestered between the slopes of Mount Scott and Scouters Mountain. That all changed when it became the fastest-growing city in Oregon. It drastically transformed into an expanding, busy, suburban city of subdivisions and commercial businesses. Happy Valley went from being an almost completely unknown community to one of the most popular places to live in the Portland metro area. Despite Happy Valley being a small town no more, it has maintained its reputation as a special place to live.

With the city's increase in size, there have been an increase in big events. The most important day of the year on the city calendar is perhaps the Fourth of July Festival. It began in 1956, when the Happy Valley Fire District began sponsoring a Fourth of July fireworks show to raise funds for firefighting equipment. The volunteer firefighters went door to door collecting donations and then launched fireworks for the community to enjoy.[368] Eventually, the City of Happy Valley took charge of the July Fourth show, and it became an event that attracted visitors from outside the valley. The event grew over the years into the biggest day of the year in the city with a family festival at Happy Valley Park with a parade, games, music and, of course, a fireworks show. Speaking of music, the city has presented entertainment for its residents and visitors with successful and popular series of summer concerts at Happy Valley Park and at the Village Green Park by the Happy Valley Library.

Happy Valley City Hall in 2014. *Bud Unruh.*

A successful music event came to Happy Valley in 2006 when the Pickathon Music Festival relocated to the Pendarvis family farm in Happy Valley by Hagen Road.[369] William Pendarvis, also known as "Bill," was born in Oklahoma in 1924. His work for William Volker and Company brought him to Portland, Oregon, where he met Betty Luckey, and they married in 1952. Betty was born in Portland to Charles and Lillian Luckey, and they moved to the Happy Valley area in the 1940s to a farm by 162nd Avenue. Bill and Betty had filbert trees on their property, but when the trees became diseased, they decided to replace them with something new.[370] In the 1990s, the family started growing grapes and operating a vineyard, with the grapes going to Eugene Wine Cellars in Eugene, Oregon, to make pinot noir.[371] In 2006, Bill and Betty's kids brought the Pickathon festival to the family farm. The music festival had previously spent six years at Horning's Hideout in Washington County and one year at the Pudding River Festival Grounds in Woodburn before relocating to Happy Valley.[372] William Pendarvis passed away in 2017 in Happy Valley.

With Happy Valley expected to be a small town no more, a larger city hall was necessary. On November 24, 2008, the city hall on 162nd Avenue and Misty Drive opened to the public.[373] The building was gigantic compared to the old city hall building that was built to resemble the old Rebstock family farmhouse. The deluxe and spacious twenty-first-century structure became a symbol of Happy Valley's expansionist efforts, as more room was desperately needed for the city's expected growth into the future. With the city's growth, more medical care was needed, and the Happy Valley Providence Immediate Care Clinic opened along Sunnyside Road in 2009.[374] Another medical clinic that opened many years earlier was the Kaiser-Permanente Medical Center by Sunnyside Road. This clinic opened on September 5, 1975, and the dedication ceremony was attended by Henry Mead Kaiser, the president of Kaiser Foundation International. The keynote speaker was state treasurer James A. Redden.[375]

In an indication of its potential growth, the Sunnyside area also saw a significant addition with the Safeway anchored shopping center. In February 1985, a proposal to build a Safeway store and shopping center was approved in a two-to-one vote by the Clackamas County commissioners. The commissioners rejected an earlier proposal for the project in July 1984 after the Clackamas County Planning Commission recommended a rejection after determining the construction of the center in a residential area would have a negative impact on the neighborhood.[376] Commissioners Robert Schumacher and Ed Lindquist approved the plan after Schumacher had voted against the previous plan to build the grocery store in Sunnyside but changed his mind, as he believed the neighborhood wanted the store. A petition was signed by seven hundred people who lived within one mile of the proposed construction site at 122nd Avenue and Sunnyside Road and favored the project. Board chairman Dale Harlan, the lone dissenter among the commissioners, believed the shopping center would create worsening traffic problems along Sunnyside Road. Although the site was not within Happy Valley's city limits, the Happy Valley City Council opposed the shopping center, as they believed it was unnecessary, would cause traffic problems and would harm property values.[377] The shopping center was at the center of a debate over Sunnyside's future development. Some opposing residents thought the proposed Sunnyside site was unnecessary due to Safeway's plan to build another store in Damascus. Although some people who lived in the area viewed the project unfavorably, the Sunnyside-area residents in favor of the project informed the county commissioners they would welcome the shopping center to shorten their travel for grocery shopping. The Happy Valley City Council, North Clackamas School District, Sunnyside United Neighbors and the Rock Creek Neighborhood Association all opposed the shopping center project. The school district opposed the plan as they owned property by the proposed site and wanted to keep the possible option of building a school.[378] When the Sunnyside Marketplace, anchored by Safeway, opened in 1989, Ben Schellenberg, superintendent of the North Clackamas School District, and Chuck Hopman, principal of Sunnyside Elementary School, participated in the grand opening ceremony in an apparent about-face from the school district's earlier opposition to the development project.

The Crossroads East development under construction in July 2021. *Happy Valley History Collection.*

A major shopping center that opened in the city was the Happy Valley Crossroads anchored by grocery giant Fred Meyer. This retail and restaurant complex held a grand opening on November 4, 2016. The $80 million project was constructed on thirty-four acres at Sunnyside Road and 172nd Avenue with Fred Meyer—the largest in the state of Oregon when it opened—at its center.[379] The Crossroads complex opened the most number of businesses in Happy Valley at one time with nine in total.[380] The Crossroads East complex was then constructed across the street, and the once rural area around the Emmanuel Community Church became a commercial hub.

Although the City of Happy Valley now features many commercial and retail businesses, seeing any businesses at all was for much of its history a rare sight due to the city's reputation and persistence to remain a residential-only community. One business that existed in Happy Valley prior to the city's expansive development growth was the Happy Valley Nursery, a garden center on eight and a half acres located along 129th Avenue. Moses and Ann Karam came to Portland in 1974 from Syria. They lived in Milwaukie before moving to the Happy Valley area in 1979, living in a house near the intersection of Sunnyside Road and 122nd Avenue where a Walgreens would later be built. The Karams bought the nursery property from longtime Happy Valley city councilor Jack Kato and opened their nursery in the late 1980s. Moses worked at the Crown Zellerbach Paper Mill for twenty-one years before retiring.[381] In 2012, the nursery donated one

The Happy Valley Nursery sign along 129th Avenue. *Happy Valley History Collection.*

hundred cedar trees that were planted in the Happy Valley Park wetland and along the Mount Scott Creek Trail.[382] Although it is not a commercial or retail establishment, the nursery is unique in being a business located in the bowl when the Happy Valley City Council maintained a promise to keep the valley between Mount Scott and Scouters Mountain a residential area. The Happy Valley Preschool also found its place in the valley. The preschool and childcare center is located along 145th Avenue on the old Kanne family farm that became a boarding facility for horses owned by the Clifford Friesen family. Cliff and Mary Friesen moved in the early 1970s to Happy Valley, where they had a farmhouse and several buildings. After their daughter Rhonda earned a degree in teaching and started her own family, she and Mary decided to start their own daycare business at their property and opened the preschool in 1990.[383]

Another place that experienced drastic change was the Top O' Scott golf course. The public course opened in 1926 and was located north of Sunnyside Road on Mount Scott on land later annexed into the City of Happy Valley.[384] The 1951 Oregon Open golf championship was played at the Top O' Scott course and was won by John Langford.[385] In 1987, the nearby New Hope Community Church purchased the property and sold off some of the course's acreage, which was then developed into commercial buildings, and the change in scenery contributed to Top O' Scott losing its charming popularity. In the 1990s, West Linn developer Neil Nedelisky purchased the Top O' Scott property, and ambitious plans of transforming the site to include business offices, homes and apartment buildings was proposed. The Top O' Scott course closed in 2003 and was converted into a pitch-and-putt par three course called Eagle Landing, which opened in 2004. A glorious bronze statue of an eagle was erected at the entrance to the Eagle Landing development and is an unmissable work of art along Stevens Road.[386]

When Happy Valley incorporated in 1965, the small city depended on the Clackamas County Sheriff's Office for law enforcement. In the early 2000s, after Happy Valley's transformation into a bigger town began, the city paid the sheriff's office to have a dedicated deputy patrol Happy Valley. In 2002, residents considered creating their own police force. The sheriff's office crime statistics at the time showed that Happy Valley had the lowest crime rate of any city in the county at less than 2 percent of annual reported crimes. Despite this fact, several of the city's homeowner associations formed neighborhood watch programs and realized the city was only going to increase in population, and with it would come an increase in crime.[387] In the November 2002 election, a levy to create a dedicated police force passed with 1,375 to 1,011 votes.[388] The levy idea emerged from a group of neighbors who created the Traffic and Public Safety Committee, which advised the Happy Valley City Council.[389] The successful levy allowed the city to hire four police officers through a contract with the Clackamas County Sheriff's Office. In 2009, the former city hall on King Road became the Happy Valley Policing Center.[390]

With Happy Valley expanding into the Sunnyside area, the city was finally able to build a library. The Happy Valley Library originally opened as the Sunnyside branch of the Clackamas County Library in 2012 to replace the Clackamas Corner branch near the northeast corner of Clackamas Town Center. The Clackamas Corner Library had become crowded and was in need of additional space.[391] The Sunnyside Village Community Center along Sieben Park Way south of Sunnyside Road was selected to be remodeled into the new library, which was previously being leased by the North Clackamas School District.[392] The county later transferred the library to the City of Happy Valley in 2015. Also in 2015, just a quick walk

The Happy Valley Station opening on November 18, 2015, with Station owner Valerie Hunter cutting the ribbon with Mayor Chavez-DeRemer. *City of Happy Valley.*

from the library, the growing city added another amenity with the Happy Valley Station food carts. Station owner Valerie Hunter and Mayor Lori Chavez-DeRemer cut the ribbon at the opening ceremony for the station on November 18, 2015.[393]

In addition to the evangelical church at 129th Avenue and Mount Scott Boulevard and the Sunnyside Community Church formerly at 122nd Avenue and Sunnyside Road, the Happy Valley area has seen a number of other churches be planted to serve the growing population. These churches include the Happy Valley Baptist Church in the bowl along King Road. The church first began meeting in the home of Bill and Sue Powers in Happy Valley. As the congregation grew, they began meeting in the clubhouse at the Top O' Scott golf course until the first church building opened in 1969 with Leonard Martin as pastor. When the North Clackamas School District planned on constructing the new Happy Valley Elementary and Middle School buildings in 2006, they needed the property the church was located on. The school district took the land, and in exchange, the church got the land immediately to the east for a new building. The newly built Happy Valley Baptist Church opened in 2009.[394]

On Mount Scott, the New Hope Community Church was started by Dale and Margi Galloway in 1972. New Hope emerged from the Galloways' dream of building "a church for the unchurched thousands" of the Portland area.[395] The church congregation met in rented facilities until 1980, when it moved to the location on Stevens Road just north of Sunnyside Road. In 1987, the 2,700-seat worship center was completed and became a landmark overlooking Interstate 205. The nondenominational church became one of Oregon's largest, with about six thousand members in the 2000s.[396] In 2020, New Hope sold the church building and property for more than $13 million to the Vietnamese Catholic community, and the building became Our Lady of La Vang Catholic Church.[397] The New Hope congregation then relocated to a new location on the north side of Mount Scott. Also on Mount Scott is the Sunnyside Church of the Nazarene. In 1991, Pastor Don Harris and his wife, Gail, sought to plant a church in the Sunnyside area. Pastor Harris visited the Mount Scott Elementary School to inquire about holding services there. After first being rejected, he began to leave the school when he was stopped and asked if the cafeteria would be suitable. He agreed, and the first service for Sunnyside Church of the Nazarene was held on March 29, 1992. The church purchased nearby land to construct their own building on 92nd Avenue that opened in 2001.[398]

Other churches in the Happy Valley area include the Creator Lutheran Church along Sunnyside Road. In 1987, Reverend David Hungerford started a new congregation that held its first worship service in the Sunnyside Elementary School gym. In 1993, Creator Lutheran started construction for its own building. The new church building opened in 1994 across the street from Sunnyside Elementary.[399] Across the road from Creator Lutheran is the Sunnyside Foursquare Church. This congregation first began meeting at the Sunnyside Motel, then worshiped at Sunnyside Elementary School for a few years and finally moved across Sunnyside Road into its own building in 1984.[400] They have also been referred to as simply the Sunnyside Church. Down Sunnyside Road to the east is a historic church building at 172nd Avenue called the Emmanuel Community Church. The church was once the Rock Creek School. The schoolhouse was purchased by the Valley Chapel Conservative Baptist Church in the 1950s and was renovated for the congregation. In the 1970s, an additional wing was built. In 1988, Valley Chapel merged with another church congregation to create the new Emmanuel Community Church.[401]

Happy Valley is no longer a small town. It never really looked like a town to begin with. It was more like a neighborhood or a small community of neighbors where everyone knew everyone's name, car and house. Happy Valley experienced an incredible transformation from its increase in size

Overlooking the valley bowl from Mount Scott in 2015. *Bud Unruh.*

and amount of events, to building a more expansive city hall, opening new medical facilities, welcoming a variety of new businesses, constructing retail complexes, expanding emergency services and more community meeting places. The city is no longer the small, isolated rural place of its beginnings. Its identity began to change dramatically in the late twentieth century. Although this change became irreversible, there are some things that have not been forgotten. Happy Valley is a great place to live because it's a special place. It has managed to keep its individuality and the smaller community feeling of the old days. It's beautiful and unique. This is not just a place to live. It's home. That's why I and so many others love the special place that is the City of Happy Valley.

Appendix

A CHRONOLOGY OF
HAPPY VALLEY, OREGON

1851
Christian and Matilda Deardorff settle on a donation land claim by Scouters Mountain and are the first American pioneers to settle in what would become Happy Valley.

October 1851
John M. Deardorff claims 320 acres next to his parents' claim.

1852
Francis and Amanda Talbert and their children travel the Oregon Trail and arrive in Oregon. Francis receives a donation land claim in Happy Valley. Francis's son John A. Talbert serves in many public positions, including in the state legislature. Mount Talbert was likely named after the family.

1858
The historic Deardorff barn is constructed on the property of John M. Deardorff.

January 6, 1876
A traveled road going from Harmony to Damascus is established as County Road #96. This road would later be named Southeast Sunnyside Road.

1884

The Sunnyside School is established at the northeast corner of 122nd Avenue and Sunnyside Road.

December 14, 1884

Christian Deardorff, patriarch of the first family to settle in Happy Valley, passes away and is buried in the Deardorff Pioneer Cemetery on Scouters Mountain.

December 17, 1888

The Sunnyside Post Office is established with John R. Welch as postmaster.

1890

John George, John Chris and Charles Frederick Zinser each build homes in Happy Valley, and the Zinser family becomes one of the longest-residing families in the community.

April 30, 1891

Matilda Deardorff, the matriarch of the first family to settle in Happy Valley, passes away and is buried in the Deardorff Pioneer Cemetery.

1892

A small one-room schoolhouse opens on land donated to the county from John M. Deardorff's land claim. It will be known as the Christilla School.

1898

The area going north to Foster Road is surveyed for a new county road. This would be an important route for valley residents to reach the markets on Foster Road. This road would become known as 132nd Avenue on the Clackamas County side and Deardorff Road on the Multnomah County side.

1901

George Zinser sells his house to Karl Charles Rebstock and moves to California. The home would become known as the Rebstock house and was located on the site of the Happy Valley Policing Center.

1902

In a meeting at the school, a new name for the valley is selected to be "Christilla Valley" to honor Christian (Chris) and Matilda (Tilla) Deardorff.

December 7, 1902
John M. Deardorff passes away and is buried in the Deardorff Pioneer Cemetery.

1908
A farmer's telephone line is installed, providing telephone communication in Happy Valley with the outside world.

1908
Frank Ott opens a feed mill on Sunnyside Road. Ott and his wife, Louise, would also open the adjoining Sunnyside Country Store, a popular stop for Happy Valley–area residents.

May 17, 1911
Ed Rebstock is born in Happy Valley. Ed helped build many of Happy Valley's roads, string its telephone lines, install its water system, organize the fire district, serve on the board of directors for the elementary school and was known as "Mr. Happy Valley."

March 1916
A severe windstorm hits rural Clackamas County. William Marks, a rancher in Happy Valley, was killed when a huge tree fell across the kitchen in his house, pinning him to the floor. His wife and daughter were inside at the time but escaped. A possible tornado was believed to have occurred.[402]

1917
The Christilla School in the valley bowl is replaced by a larger schoolhouse on the same site. This structure would later become the music room when the school expanded.

1925
Happy Valley's first paved road is constructed.

1925
Happy Valley receives electricity.

1926
Top O' Scott golf course, located near Stevens Road on Mount Scott, opens.

July 19, 1930
The Mount Scott Water District is officially incorporated by the State of Oregon. It will later become the Sunrise Water Authority.

1946
A central water system is installed in Happy Valley.

1949
Happy Valley Fire District No. 65 is formed by volunteers.

1949
Sunnyside Elementary School is dedicated.

1949
Wally Hubbard and his brothers build a concrete dam on his property along Sieben Creek. Wally's swimming hole will become a popular attraction in the Sunnyside area.

February 1951
Blaine Clayton Van Ausdeln, a World War I veteran, is the first person to be buried in the new Willamette National Cemetery on Mount Scott.

1954
East Mount Scott School patrons vote thirty-four to three to change the name of the school to Happy Valley School.

1955
Construction begins for a Boy Scouts lodge on Scouters Mountain. It opened in 1956 and was formally dedicated in 1957. It was later named the Chief Obie Lodge for George Oberteuffer, who established the training center there.

1956
The Happy Valley Fire Department begins sponsoring a Fourth of July fireworks show.

November 14, 1957
Clackamas High School on Webster Road is dedicated, which Happy Valley students will attend.

1958

The community comes together and helps in the construction of the Happy Valley Fire Station on King Road.

1960

A new large brick building is constructed at Happy Valley Elementary School. The north section containing the fifth- and sixth-grade classrooms would be added in 1967.

October 1962

The Columbus Day Storm hits Happy Valley and the Pacific Northwest. Scientifically called a typhoon, the 1962 Columbus Day Storm was a hurricane-like weather event that downed trees, blocked roads, damaged homes and barns and knocked out electricity for several days in Happy Valley. Noreen Sample, a resident who lived through the event, concluded that "a hurricane did pass through Happy Valley that day."[403]

1963

A portion of the property of Robert and Doris Francis is purchased by the Mount Scott Investment Group for the purpose of creating a park. More property would be purchased, and the land would become Happy Valley Park.

August 25, 1965

Happy Valley residents vote 111 to 66 in favor of incorporation, and the vote is certified by the Board of Clackamas County Commissioners. Happy Valley becomes Clackamas County's eleventh municipality and the first since 1913.

November 17, 1965

The first Happy Valley City Council meeting takes place at the Happy Valley Fire Station. James Robnett becomes Happy Valley's first mayor at the meeting.

1970

Happy Valley population is 1,392.

1980

Happy Valley population is 1,499.

1980
Ash from the eruption of Mount St. Helens lands in Happy Valley.

March 6, 1981
The Clackamas Town Center shopping mall opens.

1982
The Cedar Creek Crossing Covered Bridge along Deardorff Road opens. The bridge replaced a deteriorating one built in 1936, which itself replaced the first bridge that was built in the 1880s.

1984
Ed Rebstock, "Mr. Happy Valley," passes away.

1989
The Mount Scott Elementary School opens.

1990
Happy Valley population is 1,519.

1991
The historic Rebstock house, built in 1890, is demolished. The house was intended to be renovated and become the new city hall. The city offices at that time were located across the street in the same building as the Mount Scott Water District. The house was torn down due to termite damage, and a new building in the style of an old farmhouse was constructed and became the city hall.

January 1995
The city council selects Randy Nicolay to become Happy Valley's second mayor, ending James Robnett's nearly thirty-year tenure as the city's first mayor.

1997
The historic Deardorff barn is torn down to make way for the Happy Valley Heights subdivision.

January 1999

The city council selects Eugene Grant to be Happy Valley's third mayor. During his tenure, Grant oversaw the development and expansion by annexation of the city. Grant holds the distinction of being the last mayor chosen by city council and the first elected by voters after a new city charter went into effect.[404]

2000

Happy Valley population is 4,519, a 197.5 percent increase from 1990.

2000

The Spring Mountain Elementary School opens.

November 9, 2000

Sunrise Water Authority is established from the Mount Scott and Damascus Water Districts.

April 3, 2002

Students move into the new Clackamas High School building on 122nd Avenue in Clackamas.

2004

The Chief Obie Lodge is closed by the state fire marshal due to it being a fire hazard.

2006

Happy Valley is issued its own zip code from the U.S. Postal Service.[405]

2006

The Pickathon Music Festival relocates to the Pendarvis farm.

January 2007

Rob Wheeler, a city council member for six years, becomes Happy Valley's fourth mayor.[406]

October 6, 2007

Mount Talbert Nature Park has its grand opening.

May 10, 2008

Happy Valley's first and longtime mayor James Robnett passes away.

2008

The old Happy Valley Elementary School building is torn down, and the new elementary and middle school buildings are constructed.

November 24, 2008

The Happy Valley City Hall on Misty Drive opens.

2009

The former city hall becomes the Happy Valley Policing Center.

2009

Happy Valley Middle School opens.

2009

Scouters Mountain Elementary School opens.

2009

Verne A. Duncan Elementary School opens.

September 12, 2009

The first MAX Light Rail Line to extend into Clackamas County, the Green Line, opens to the public at Clackamas Town Center.

2010

Happy Valley population is 13,903, a 207.7 percent increase from 2000.

2010

Rock Creek Middle School opens.

January 2011

Lori Chavez-DeRemer becomes Happy Valley's fifth mayor. She and her husband founded Anesthesia Associates Northwest, a healthcare firm. Prior to being elected mayor, she served on the Happy Valley Parks Committee and on city council.[407]

2011
The Chief Obie Lodge on Scouters Mountain is deconstructed.

2012
The Sunnyside Library, later renamed the Happy Valley Library, opens. It replaced the Clackamas Corner Library by Clackamas Town Center.

December 11, 2012
A shooting rampage at Clackamas Town Center takes the lives of Cindy Ann Yuille and Steven Forsyth.

2013
The skate park at Happy Valley Park opens.

August 28, 2014
Scouters Mountain Nature Park opens.

November 18, 2015
Happy Valley Station food carts open.

November 4, 2016
Happy Valley Crossroads retail and restaurant development, anchored by Fred Meyer, opens at Sunnyside Road and 172nd Avenue.

May 26, 2017
Happy Valley resident and army veteran Ricky Best defends two girls from a racist attack aboard a TriMet MAX train and dies from his injuries.

January 2019
Tom Ellis, a U.S. Coast Guard veteran, becomes Happy Valley's sixth mayor. After moving to Happy Valley, he served on the Planning Commission for six years. He was appointed and then elected to city council before being elected as mayor.[408]

2019
Hidden Falls Nature Park opens.

2019
Beatrice Morrow Cannady Elementary School opens.

2020
Happy Valley's population is 23,733, a 70.7 percent increase from 2010.

March 2020
The COVID-19 pandemic begins to impact Happy Valley.

June 3, 2020
Black Lives Matter protesters march along Sunnyside Road from Clackamas High School to Happy Valley City Hall.

July 2020
Happy Valley Parks and Recreation District opens its first season of programming.

2020
David Emami becomes the first Iranian American city councilor elected in Oregon. He was previously appointed to the Happy Valley City Council to fill the seat vacated when Tom Ellis became mayor.[409]

2021
Adrienne C. Nelson High School, the first high school in Happy Valley city limits, opens.

November 2022
Former Happy Valley mayor Lori Chavez-DeRemer is elected to represent Oregon's fifth congressional district in the U.S. House of Representatives.

NOTES

Introduction

1. *Oregonian*, April 21, 1966, 43.

Chapter 1

2. Bishop, *In Search of Ancient Oregon*, 189, 214–15.
3. "Kellogg Creek, Mt Scott Creek," Urban Streams Council.
4. "Rock Creek Comprehensive Plan," City of Happy Valley, 14.
5. "Discover Rock Creek: Home of the Happy Fish of Happy Valley," *Happy Valley Monthly*, November 2014.
6. Fegel, *History of Happy Valley*, 2; Sample, "Happy Valley as I Remember It."
7. Fegel, *History of Happy Valley*, 1–2; Knause, interview; Simina Mistreanu, "A," *Oregonian*, July 10, 2014; Katherine Kisiel, "Cougar Prowls Outside Happy Valley Home," Katu.com, May 5, 2022.
8. Fegel, *History of Happy Valley*, 1–2; Sample, "As I Remember It."

Chapter 2

9. Ruby, *Guide to the Indian Tribes of the Pacific Northwest*, 25–26.
10. Beckham, *Indians of Western Oregon*, 52.

11. Confederated Tribes of Grand Ronde, *Chinuk Wawa*, 137.
12. Ruby, *Guide to the Indian Tribes of the Pacific Northwest*, 25–26.
13. Courtnier, "Mt. Talbert Cave."
14. *Portrait and Biographical Record of Portland*, 415.
15. Ibid.
16. Cockle and Deardorff, interview.
17. Oregon donation land claim applications, vol. 2.
18. Deardorff Cockle, interview.
19. Fegel, *History of Happy Valley*, 16.
20. Cockle and Deardorff, interview.
21. *Portrait and Biographical Record of Portland*, 415–16.
22. Clackamas County Historic Resources Inventory, 1989–92.
23. Cockle and Deardorff, interview.
24. Deardorff Huddle, "Old Home Place."
25. Deardorff Cockle, "Some Memories of Childhood Days."
26. County Road 641, 149; Verda Spickelmeier, "Deardorffs Part of Happy Valley's Colorful Past," *Clackamas County Review*, June 19, 1991; Paul Pintarich, "New Covered Bridge Anachronism Spanning Johnson Creek," *Oregonian*, January 5, 1982.
27. Deardorff Cockle, "Some Memories of Childhood Days."
28. "School Fund Apportionment," *Oregon City Enterprise*, April 22, 1892.
29. Fegel, *History of Happy Valley*, 19.
30. *Portrait and Biographical Record of Portland*, 415–16.

Chapter 3

31. H.W. Kanne, "East Mt. Scott," *Oregon City Enterprise*, February 9, 1912, 2.
32. Strickrott, interview.
33. Fegel, *History of Happy Valley*, 7.
34. Oregon, U.S., Naturalization Records 1865–1991.
35. "Happy Valley: A Pathway to the Past," Happy Valley Elementary School.
36. 1920 United States Census.
37. Steven Amick, "Old Barn to Be Razed to Build Subdivision," *Oregonian*, July 25, 1997.
38. *Oregonian*, August 14, 2002.
39. 1920 United States Census.
40. Sample, "As I Remember It."
41. Zinser, "Zinser Family."

42. *Oregon City Enterprise*, May 11, 1900, 2.

43. Zinser, "Zinser Family."

44. Zinser, "Happy Valley and Zinser Family Memories"; Zinser, "Zinser Family."

45. *Portrait and Biographical Record of Portland*, 382.

46. *Morning Enterprise,* June 10, 1925.

47. Zinser, "Zinser Family."

48. Zinser, "Happy Valley and Zinser Family Memories."

49. Cindy Free-Fetty, "Penny Mead, 91, Reminisces about 81 Years in the Community," *Happy Valley Monthly*, March 2015.

50. Deardorff Huddle, "Old Home Place."

51. Fegel, *History of Happy Valley*, 8.

52. Deardorff Huddle, "Old Home Place."

53. Fegel, *History of Happy Valley*, 8; Cockle and Deardorff, interview.

54. Fegel, *History of Happy Valley*, 7–8.

55. Ibid.

56. Ulrich Ott, interview.

57. Kanne, "East Mt. Scott," 2.

58. Fegel, *History of Happy Valley*, 7–8; Peterson, interview.

59. *Oregon City Enterprise*, September 14, 1906, 2.

60. Fegel, *History of Happy Valley*, 7–8; Peterson, interview.

61. Eisert, interview.

62. Fegel, *History of Happy Valley*, 9–10.

63. Kanne, "East Mt. Scott," 2.

64. "History of Planning for Happy Valley," City of Happy Valley; Lynda Lesowski, "Rural Happy Valley Wants to Stay that Way," *Oregon Journal*, June 22, 1982, 35.

Chapter 4

65. Metsker's Atlas of Clackamas County, 1937.

66. General Land Office Records, Bureau of Land Management; Clackamas County Clerk Tax Assessor Maps, Clackamas County, Oregon.

67. Early Oregonians Index; 1880 United States Census.

68. Hines, *Illustrated History of the State of Oregon*; Ryckman, *Grandma, You Were a Daisy!*

69. Ryckman, *Grandma, You Were A Daisy!*

70. *Morning Oregonian*, December 28, 1900.

71. Hines, *Illustrated History of the State of Oregon*; "Amanda Talbert Dead," *Oregon City Enterprise*, April 27, 1900.
72. *Weekly Enterprise*, January 18, 1929.
73. *Morning Oregonian*, December 28, 1900.
74. *Morning Oregonian*, January 15, 1929.
75. Fred Lockley, *Oregon Journal*, April 6, 1937.
76. Hines, *Illustrated History of the State of Oregon*.
77. Lockley, *Oregon Journal*, April 6, 1937.
78. *Oregon City Courier*, September 9, 1915.
79. *Oregon City Courier*, March 6, 1896.
80. McArthur, *Oregon Geographic Names*.

Chapter 5

81. Hubbard Cook, interview.
82. Register of County Roads, Road No. 96, Clackamas County, Oregon.
83. Board of County Commissioners Court Order No. 72-302, March 22, 1972.
84. Ott, interview.
85. Hubbard Cook, interview.
86. *Morning Enterprise*, June 9, 1912, 3.
87. LaPontic, interview.
88. "The Sunnyside Community History," Sandy Van Bemmel; Jo Ann Boatwright, *Clackamas County Review*, July 29, 1992.
89. McArthur, *Oregon Geographic Names*, 924.
90. Ott, interview.
91. *Oregon City Enterprise*, July 24, 1908.
92. *Morning Enterprise*, May 28, 1912, 3.
93. Ott, "History of the Ott Family."
94. Jim Kadera, "Sunnyside Commons Keeps Spirit of Farm Era Alive," *Oregonian*, July 31, 1997, 5.
95. *Clackamas County Cultural Resource Inventory*, Clackamas County Policy and Project Development Division, 1984.
96. Ott Piper, interview.
97. "Getting There," Clackamas County Department of Transportation and Development, 1995.
98. Ott Piper, interview.
99. Hubbard, interview.

100. *Oregon Journal*, October 16, 1911, 13.

101. Walter Hubbard journal.

102. Ashton, "Children Born to Walter and Alma Hubbard."

103. Hubbard, interview.

104. *Oregon City Enterprise*, July 6, 1906, 2.

105. Hubbard Cook, interview, 1997.

106. *Oregonian*, May 24, 1981, 121.

107. *Oregonian*, February 21, 1964, 25; Adolf Gutknecht World War II Registration card; 1930 United States Census.

108. "Sunnyside Community History," Van Bemmel, 1997.

109. *Sunnyside School Centennial*.

110. Nancy Haught, "Another Resurrection," *Oregonian*, March 27, 2005.

111. Raymond Rendleman, "New Happy Valley Sign to Greet Sunnyside Road Drivers," *Clackamas Review*, January 9, 2013.

112. "Sunnyside Community History," Van Bemmel, 1997; *Clackamas County Cultural Resource Inventory*, Clackamas County Policy and Project Development Division, 1984.

113. Cindy Free-Fetty, "Penny Mead, 91, Reminisces about 81 Years in the Community," *Happy Valley Monthly*, March 2015.

114. *Oregon City Enterprise*, June 8, 1906, 2.

115. Grischow, interview.

116. "Happy Valley Comprehensive Plan," City of Happy Valley, May 5, 2009; *Clackamas County Cultural Resource Inventory*, 1984.

117. Ulrich Ott, interview.

118. Orme, interview.

Chapter 6

119. Ott, "History of the Ott Family."

120. *Oregon City Enterprise*, July 24, 1908.

121. Ott, interview.

122. *Morning Enterprise*, May 28, 1912, 3.

123. Ott Piper, interview.

124. Elisabeth Purse, "Country Store Retains Charm," *Oregon Journal*, March 4, 1980, 44.

125. *Oregon Journal*, April 27, 1974, 9.

126. Hubbard, interview.

127. Jim Kadera, "Sunnyside Commons Keeps Spirit of Farm Era Alive," *Oregonian*, July 31, 1997, 5.

128. Jim Kadera, "Sunnyside Commons Lands More History," *Oregonian*, September 27, 2001, 4.

129. *Clackamas County Cultural Resource Inventory*, 1984.

130. Sarah Hunsberger, "Old Barn in Path of Road Project," *Oregonian*, February 10, 2005, 1.

131. *Oregonian*, April 26, 1974, 50.

Chapter 7

132. Fegel, *History of Happy Valley*, 11.

133. Knause, interview.

134. "A Pathway to the Past," 1992; Cockle and Deardorff, interview.

135. Kanne, "East Mt. Scott," 2.

136. County Road 641.

137. Paul Pintarich, "New Covered Bridge Anachronism Spanning Johnson Creek," *Oregonian*, January 5, 1982.

138. Cockle and Deardorff, interview; Fegel, *History of Happy Valley*.

139. Clackamas County Surveyor's Map, 1926.

140. *Oregon City Enterprise*, April 14, 1922.

141. Fegel, *History of Happy Valley*, 11.

142. *Oregon Journal*, March 20, 1927, 51.

143. *Morning Oregonian*, June 15, 1908; Peterson, "Happy Valley History."

144. Fegel, *History of Happy Valley*, 11–12.

145. "Sunnyside Community History," Van Bemmel, 1997.

146. Monner, interview; *Oregonian*, February 9, 1972, 26.

147. Mount Scott Water District, "Articles of Incorporation," Sunrise Water Authority, Happy Valley, OR, 1930.

148. Sample, "As I Remember It."

149. Fegel, *History of Happy Valley*, 12; "History of Planning for Happy Valley," City of Happy Valley.

150. Minutes and records, Sunrise Water Authority, Happy Valley, OR. 2000.

151. Sample, "As I Remember It."

152. Shelley McFarland, "Forged in Love, a Son's Tribute to His Father," *Happy Valley News*, August 2021.

153. Sample, "As I Remember It."

154. Beutler, interview.

155. *Oregon Journal*, October 12, 1967, 10.

156. Michael Wade, "Clackamas 71 Oks Fire District Merger," *Oregonian*, December 16, 1988, E18.
157. Kanne, "East Mt. Scott," 2.
158. Fegel, *History of Happy Valley*, 15; Sample, "As I Remember It"; *Oregon Daily Journal*, February 14, 1915, 13.
159. Sample, "As I Remember It."

Chapter 8

160. Fegel, *History of Happy Valley*, 18–19; Strickrott, interview.
161. Fegel, *History of Happy Valley*, 18–19.
162. Peterson, interview; Eisert, interview.
163. Fegel, *History of Happy Valley*, 18–19.
164. Eisert, interview.
165. A. Zinser, interview.
166. Geppert, interview.
167. "Valley Bell Back Home," newspaper account; D. Zinser, interview.
168. Fegel, *History of Happy Valley*, 18–19.
169. Geppert, interview.
170. *Oregonian*, July 2, 1954.
171. Fegel, *History of Happy Valley*, 18–19.
172. Mrs. Ed Rebstock, interview.
173. A. Zinser, interview; Mrs. Ed Rebstock, interview.
174. Kochendorfer, interview.
175. Mrs. Ed Rebstock, interview.
176. Ulrich Ott, interview.
177. Peterson, interview.
178. Hubbard Ulrich, interview; Orme, interview.
179. Yim Su-jin, "Record-Setting 2006 Bond Allows Districtwide Rehab," *Oregonian*, September 17, 2009; Dennis McCarthy, "Happy Valley's Schools Could Benefit from Levy," *Oregonian*, September 28, 2006.
180. *Sunnyside School Centennial*, 1.
181. Ott, interview.
182. *Sunnyside School Centennial*, 2.
183. Hubbard Cook, interview; Hubbard Ulrich, interview.
184. *Sunnyside School Centennial*, 4–5.
185. Ibid., 6.
186. Ibid., 7–8.

187. *The New Review*, September 12, 1979.

188. "Community Link," North Clackamas Schools, Fall 2019.

189. LaPontic, interview.

190. Grischow, interview.

191. *Oregon City Courier*, February 23, 1906, 3; *Oregon City Courier*, April 5, 1917, 6.

192. Grischow, interview.

193. *Oregonian*, November 15, 1957, 26.

194. "First Day of School," *Oregonian*, April 4, 2002.

195. *Clackamas County Review*, September 1989.

196. "Mount Scott Elementary School Profile 2000–2001," North Clackamas School District.

197. *Oregonian*, August 31, 2000, 1.

198. Su-jin, "Record-Setting 2006 Bond."

199. Yim Su-jin, "North Clackamas' New Clothes," *Oregonian*, September 17, 2009.

200. "Sunrise Middle School Profile 2005–2006," North Clackamas School District.

201. Shelley McFarland, "New School Year in New Digs," *Happy Valley News*, October 2019.

202. "Community Link," North Clackamas School District, Fall 2019; Raymond Rendleman, "NCSD Names Beatrice Cannady Elementary School," *Clackamas Review*, May 16, 2018.

203. Rendleman, "NCSD Names Beatrice Cannady Elementary School."

204. Raymond Rendleman, "North Clackamas High School Naming, Part 2," *Clackamas Review*, February 7, 2019; Raymond Rendleman, "North Clackamas High School Named for Justice Adrienne Nelson," *Clackamas Review*, May 13, 2019.

205. Shelley McFarland, "Adrienne Nelson Aims to Inspire Students at New High School," *Happy Valley News*, August 2021.

206. Jaelen Ogadhoh, "A Supremely Grand Opening," *Clackamas Review*, August 25, 2021.

Chapter 9

207. Fegel, *History of Happy Valley*, 19.

208. "Unique Farming Community in the Environs of Portland," *Sunday Oregonian*, September 5, 1948.

209. Witter, *Place Names in Clackamas County*, 21–22.

210. "Name Selected in Honor of Pioneer Settlers Near Mount Scott," *Sunday Oregonian*, November 16, 1902.

211. *Morning Oregonian*, September 25, 1909, 11; *Sunday Oregonian*, October 17, 1909, 7.

212. "None Dead in Clackamas," *Morning Oregonian*, September 16, 1902.

213. "Smoke Is Lifting," *Oregonian*, September 16, 1904.

214. "Coyotes Show Teeth to Farmers," *Morning Oregonian*, November 2, 1904.

215. *Sunday Oregonian*, September 25, 1932.

216. *Oregonian*, July 2, 1954.

Chapter 10

217. United States Germans to America Index, ancestry.com.

218. "Warranty Deed from J. George Zinser and wife to Charles Rebstock and Bertha Rebstock"; "Warranty Deed from J.B. Deardorff and Wife to J. George Zinser."

219. Steven Amick, "Helping Other Folks Is Just a Way of Life for 'Mr. Happy Valley,'" *Oregonian*, January 23, 1984.

220. 1930 United States Census; "Erma Lydia Rebstock Obituary," *Oregonian*, September 18, 1993.

221. Amick, "Helping Other Folks"; "'Mr. Happy Valley' Dies of Cancer," *Oregonian*, April 15, 1984.

222. Lynda Lesowski, "Rural Happy Valley Wants to Stay That Way," *Oregon Journal*, June 22, 1982, 35.

223. "Ed Rebstock Honored for Service," *Clackamas County The Citizen*, June 27, 1979.

224. Lesowski, "Rural Happy Valley," 35.

225. Sample, "As I Remember It."

226. Ed Rebstock Retirement Reception, flier, Mount Scott Water District, 1979.

227. Gustafsson, interview.

228. Mrs. Ed Rebstock, interview.

229. Karl Rebstock, interview.

230. Gustafsson, interview.

231. Beutler, interview.

232. *Sunday Oregonian*, November 13, 1904, 10.

233. Gustafsson, interview.

234. "Happy Valley's Efforts to Build a City Hall Meets Dry Rot," *Inside Happy Valley*, September 1991.
235. City of Happy Valley Resolution No. 94-12, September 6, 1994.

Chapter 11

236. "Happy Valley Mayor Tells Chamber How His Suburb Won Race with City," *Oregonian*, March 17, 1966.
237. Sample, "As I Remember It."
238. "Oregon's Newest City Different in Many Ways," *Oregonian*, August 28, 1965.
239. "Village Asks City Status," *Oregonian*, August 26, 1965.
240. "Oregon's Newest City Different in Many Ways," *Oregonian*.
241. *Oregonian*, March 21, 1966, 26.
242. *Oregonian*, March 29, 1966, 18.
243. Lesowski, "Rural Happy Valley," 35.
244. "Happy Valley Elects Council," *Oregonian*, November 10, 1965.
245. "Happy Valley Council Meeting Minutes," November 17, 1965.
246. Sandra McDonough, "Tax Break, Life in Country Make Happy Valley Residents Happy," *Oregonian*, June 12, 1977, 70.

Chapter 12

247. James John Robnett, World War II Draft Card, 1944.
248. Kate Taylor, "Allies, Foes Alike Recall Former Mayor Fondly," *Oregonian*, May 22, 2008; James J. Robnett obituary, *Oregonian*, May 15, 2008.
249. Connie Potter, "Happy Valley Mayor, Values Constant," *Oregonian*, January 22, 1987.
250. Vince Kohler, "Happy Valley's Only Mayor Gets the Boot," *Oregonian*, January 12, 1995.
251. "A Tribute to a Long Time Mayor," *League of Oregon Cities Newsletter*, February 1992.
252. James J. Robnett obituary, *Oregonian*, May 15, 2008.
253. Taylor, "Allies, Foes Alike."
254. *Oregonian*, November 22, 1977.
255. Potter, "Happy Valley Mayor."
256. Coats, interview.

257. Kohler, "Happy Valley's Only Mayor."

258. Potter, "Happy Valley Mayor."

259. Taylor, "Allies, Foes Alike."

Chapter 13

260. "Tree City USA Standards," Arbor Day Foundation, www.arborday. org/programs/treecityusa/standards.

261. Smith, "Park and Field History"; Robnett, "Happy Valley Park History."

262. "A Pathway to the Past," 1992.

263. Coats, interview; Sample, "As I Remember It."

264. *Happy Valley Today*, August 2013.

265. *2020 Happy Valley Business & Community Magazine*, 10.

266. *Happy Valley Monthly*, October 2015.

267. Gustafsson, interview.

268. 1920 United States Census.

269. Sample, "As I Remember It."

270. Verda Spickelmier, "Deardorffs Part of Happy Valley's Colorful Past," *Clackamas County Review*, June 19, 1991, 7.

271. *Oregonian*, May 12, 1957, 29.

272. *Oregon Journal*, May 10, 1957, 22; Dennis McCarthy, "Happy Valley Looks to Buy Scouter Mountain Parcel," *Oregonian*, June 7, 2007.

273. *Oregon Journal*, June 25, 1961, 8.

274. *Oregon Journal*, August 26, 1980, 25.

275. *Oregon Journal*, November 8, 1980, 3; "Chief Obie's Lodge," *Oregonian*, November 7, 1980. 36.

276. Sample, "As I Remember It"; Bair, interview.

277. *Oregonian*, March 26, 1957, 33.

278. *Oregon Journal*, June 25, 1961, 8; *Oregon Journal*, August 13, 1961, 8.

279. *Oregonian*, July 23, 1968, 14.

280. "Happy Valley Teen Arraigned in Slaying," *Oregonian*, March 12, 1987, 70.

281. Steven Amick, *Oregonian*, June 10, 1987, 31.

282. *Oregonian*, July 21, 1987, 27; *Oregonian*, January 17, 1987, 35.

283. Emily Tsao, "Boy Scout Lodge Closed; Considered Fire Hazard," *Oregonian*, July 19, 2004; Emily Tsao, "Boy Scouts Told to Put Sprinklers in Lodge," *Oregonian*, July 2, 2004.

284. Yuxing Zheng, "Scouter Mountain Tract Will Become Natural Area," *Oregonian*, December 18, 2010.

285. Bair, interview.

286. Becky Shoemaker, Records Officer/Archivist, Records Information Management Services, Metro, email to author, April 4, 2019.

287. Knause, interview.

288. *Oregon Journal*, September 24, 1928, 6.

289. "New Cemetery Is Planned," *Oregonian*, October 12, 1909.

290. "Burial Plot Opens. Mount Scott Park Cemetery Is Formally Dedicated," *Oregonian*, May 31, 1912.

291. *Oregonian*, September 14, 1926; Bergen and Davis, *Historic Cemeteries of Portland*.

292. "Ladder Plunge Proves Fatal," *Oregonian*, February 13, 1951.

293. City of Happy Valley Resolution No. 94-12.

294. Shoemaker, email to author.

295. *Oregon City Enterprise*, June 8, 1906, 2.

296. "NCPRD Announces Development of Hidden Falls Park," *Clackamas Review*, August 30, 2017; Raymond Rendleman, "Community Celebrates Opening of Hidden Falls Nature Park," *Clackamas Review*, July 3, 2019.

297. Dennis McCarthy, "Next after Happy Valley Vote: Patience," *Oregonian*, May 25, 2006, 1.

298. Samantha Swindler, "Happy Valley Leaves Parks District—For parks," *Oregonian*, May 21, 2017, A2.

299. *Happy Valley Monthly*, June 2018.

300. Corlyn Voorhees, "Happy Valley Loses Approval for Parks District," *Oregonian*, June 30, 2018.

301. Raymond Rendleman, "Happy Valley, Not County, Gets Taxes for Parks," *Clackamas Review*, October 17, 2018.

302. Raymond Rendleman, "Jury Returns County Parks Funds to HV," *Clackamas Review*, August 28, 2019.

303. Raymond Rendleman, "HV, County Reach Deal on $14.3M Settlement," *Clackamas Review*, December 11, 2019.

304. "City and County Reach Settlement Agreement on Parks, Contingent on Legislation," *Happy Valley News*, January 2020.

Chapter 14

305. Wallace M. Hubbard eulogy.

306. *Oregonian*, February 3, 1966, 7; *Oregonian*, August 8, 1970, 20.

307. 1928 Metsker Maps, 11.

308. Wally Hubbard and Vernon Hubbard, interview.

309. 1940 United States Census; Amy Martinez Starke, "Wally Hubbard—Diving Deep into Life While Waiting for God," *Oregonian*, February 24, 2008, D08; *The Maroon*, vol. 22, Milwaukie, OR: Milwaukie Union High School, May 1937.

310. "Pathway to the Past"; Starke, "Wally Hubbard," D08.

311. Hubbard and Hubbard, interview; Steven Amick, "Wally's Dam Welcomes Wild Critters, Not Wild Humans," *Oregonian*, April 10, 2003, 1.

312. Wallace Hubbard, U.S., Department of Veterans Affairs BIRLS Death File, 1850–2010; Starke, "Wally Hubbard," D08.

313. Amick, "Wally's Dam Welcomes Wild Critters," 1.

314. *Oregonian*, August 12, 1976, 21.

315. Bill Keller, "Official Cites Pollution Peril at Clackamas Swimming Hole," *Oregonian*, July 20, 1971, 24; Starke, "Wally Hubbard," D08.

316. Wallace M. Hubbard eulogy.

317. Amick, "Wally's Dam Welcomes Wild Critters," 1.

318. "Sunnyside Community History," Van Bemmel.

319. Sara Wichman, "Swimming Hole Updated with 340-Foot Slide," *Oregonian*, July 16, 1971, 16; "Pathway to the Past"; Starke, "Wally Hubbard," D08; Keller, "Official Cites Pollution Peril," 24.

320. Keller, "Official Cites Pollution Peril," 24; *Oregonian*, August 6, 1969, 30.

321. *Oregonian*, August 31, 1971, 6.

322. Bill Keller, "Wally Out of Trouble; Neighbors to Fix Slide," *Oregonian*, September 10, 1971, 66.

323. Amick, "Wally's Dam Welcomes Wild Critters," 1.

324. Ibid.

325. Starke, "Wally Hubbard," D08.

326. Ibid.

Chapter 15

327. *Clackamas Review*, April 16, 1975.

328. *Oregonian*, January 26, 1995; Coats, interview.

329. *Oregonian*, September 13, 1973.

330. *Oregonian*, August 22, 1973.

331. "Clackamas Town Center Hearing Due on Development," *Oregonian*, January 20, 1975.

332. *Clackamas Review*, September 25, 1974.

333. *Oregonian*, March 18, 1975; *Clackamas Review*, March 19, 1975.

334. *Oregonian*, October 19, 1976.

335. *Oregonian*, January 26, 1995.

336. *Oregon Journal*, July 8, 1980.

337. "Town Center Heralds New Lifestyle for Area Residents," *Oregonian*, March 6, 1981; "Town Center Work to Begin," *Oregonian*, October 19, 1976.

338. *Oregonian*, August 12, 1980; "Clackamas Town Center Grand Opening," *Supplement to the Oregonian*, March 5, 1981.

339. Kate Taylor, "Library Bids Fond Adieu to Town Center," *Oregonian*, March 15, 1996.

340. Melissa L. Jones, "Skaters Take One Last Spin around Clackamas Ice Rink," *Oregonian*, April 20, 2003.

341. *Oregonian*, June 11, 2004.

342. "Thousands on MAX Go Green Festivities and Free Rides Draw Takers for the New Downtown-Clackamas Town Center Line," *Oregonian*, September 13, 2009.

343. Rick Bella, "It Was Terrifying," *Oregonian*, December 12, 2012.

344. Sam Stites, "Thousands in County Receive COVID Vaccine," *Clackamas Review*, March 31, 2021; *Clackamas Review*, September 16, 2020.

Chapter 16

345. *Oregonian*, November 22, 1977.

346. *Oregonian*, June 6, 1982.

347. Koper, interview.

348. "Land-Use Fight Ends," *Oregonian*, September 25, 1985.

349. "Sewer System Gets Little Support in Happy Valley," *Oregonian*, May 6, 1987.

350. Koper, interview.

351. Kohler, "Happy Valley's Only Mayor."

352. *Inside Happy Valley*, September 1991.

353. Taylor, "Allies, Foes Alike."

354. Mark Larabee, "Growth on the Sunnyside of Town," *Oregonian*, December 7, 1995, 1.

355. Steven Amick, "Anti-Growth Trio among 6 Seeking Happy Valley Seats," October 29, 1998.

356. Darren Freeman, "Happy Valley's Great Leap Ahead—Quality of Life, Including Good Schools, Attracts New Residents Faster Than Elsewhere in the Moderately Growing County," *Oregonian*, December 19, 2002.

357. Lesowski, "Rural Happy Valley," 35.

358. 2020 United States Census.

359. Steven Amick, "Mayor Sees 'New Day' with Happy Valley Vote < Eugene Grant Says the Annexation Ok Is a Strong Mandate That Citizens See the Benefits of Expanding," *Oregonian*, May 18, 2000.

360. "Rock Creek Comprehensive Plan," City of Happy Valley, 2001.

361. Sarah Hunsberger, "Oregon City's Mayoral Race in a Dead Heat," *Oregonian*, November 6, 2002.

362. "Happy Valley Adds 891 Acres, Hundreds of Residents," *Oregonian*, June 30, 2004, C01.

363. *Clackamas Review*, February 10, 2016.

364. Raymond Rendleman, "Local Citizens Lose Development Appeal," *Clackamas Review*, September 14, 2016.

365. Raymond Rendleman, "Entering Happy Valley—Without Moving," *Clackamas Review*, September 25, 2013.

366. Koper, interview.

367. *Oregonian*, December 19, 2002.

Chapter 17

368. Sample, "As I Remember It."

369. Lyndsey Hewitt, "Family, Known for Pickathon, Grows Pinot Noir," *Happy Valley Monthly*, April 2016; Marty Hughley, "Gettin' Down on the Farm," *Oregonian*, August 7, 2006.

370. Pendarvis, interview.

371. *Daily Oklahoman*, March 5, 2017, 20.

372. Hughley, "Gettin' Down on the Farm."

373. Kate Taylor, "South Briefs," *Oregonian*, November 13, 2008.

374. "Community News," *Oregonian*, October 1, 2009.

375. "Kaiser to Attend Opening of Clinic," *Oregonian*, September 5, 1975, 31.

376. Vince Kohler, "Panel Rejects Safeway Shopping Center in Sunnyside Area," *Oregonian*, June 13, 1984, 52.

377. Vince Kohler, "Safeway Shopping Center in Sunnyside Area Wins Approval," *Oregonian*, February 7, 1985, 40.

378. Vince Kohler, "Sunnyside Safeway Proposal Debated," *Oregonian*, January 24, 1985, 33.

379. "Happy Valley Crossroads to Open This Friday," *Clackamas Review*, November 2, 2016.

380. *Happy Valley Monthly*, November 2016.

381. Karam, interview.

382. *Happy Valley Today*, May 2012.

383. Cindy Free-Fetty, "Happy Valley Preschool Turns 25, Celebrates with Open House," *Happy Valley Monthly*, April 2015.

384. Jason Vondersmith, "It's the Final Tee for Top O' Scott," *Portland Tribune*, June 11, 2003.

385. *Oregonian*, June 21, 1951, 27.

386. Susan Hauser, "Top O' Scott Evolves from Rock Hard to New Softy," *Oregonian*, May 20, 2006, 18; Bob Robinson, "Top O' Scott Alive and Well, but Remodeling Awaits," *Oregonian*, February 14, 1999.

387. Dennis McCarthy, "Happy Valley Residents Talk of Creating Own Police Force," *Oregonian*, February 14, 2002.

388. "Election Results Clackamas County," *Oregonian*, November 14, 2002.

389. Steve Campbell, email to author, June 15, 2022.

390. City of Happy Valley records, Happy Valley City Hall.

391. Emily Fugetta, "Library Space Odyssey Gets Happy Ending," *Oregonian*, April 12, 2012.

392. *Oregonian*, February 19, 2011.

393. City of Happy Valley, facebook.com, November 18, 2015.

394. "Church History," happyvalleybaptistoregon.org/history_of_the_church.

395. "Welcome to New Hope Community Church," New Hope Community Church.

396. Timothy A. Akimoff, "New Hope Reaches Beyond Church," *Oregonian*, October 17, 2005.

397. Raymond Rendleman, "Happy Valley Megachurch Property Sold for $13.25 Million," *Clackamas Review*, June 3, 2020.

398. "Sunnyside Church of the Nazarene Dedication Service," Sunnyside Church of the Nazarene, May 6, 2001.

399. "Creator's Story," www.creatorlutheran.org.

400. John Guernsey, "Plucky Worshippers Watch Dream of New Church Reach Fruition," *Oregonian*, May 2, 1984, 37.

401. "About ECC," ecchurch.com.

Appendix

402. *Oregon City Enterprise*, March 24, 1916, 1.

403. Sample, "As I Remember It."

404. *Oregonian*, January 6, 1999.

405. *Oregonian*, June 1, 2006.

406. "Happy Valley's Next Mayor Plans to Be Part Diplomat," *Oregonian*, November 23, 2006.

407. Natalie Feulner, "Happy Valley to Make Dollars Count, Mayor Says," *Oregonian*, February 5, 2011; *Women in Business*, August 31, 2016.

408. "Happy Valley City Council Begins a New Chapter," *Happy Valley News*, February 2019; *Happy Valley Monthly*, January 2019.

409. Raymond Rendleman, "Happy Valley Election Rewrites Oregon History," *Pamplin Media Group*, November 11, 2020.

BIBLIOGRAPHY

Ashton, Verna. "Children Born to Walter and Alma Hubbard." Undated.

Bair, Dave. Interview by Mark W. Hurlburt. July 2, 2022.

Beckham, Stephen Dow. *The Indians of Western Oregon: This Land Was Theirs.* Coos Bay, OR: Arago Books, 1977.

Bergen, Teresa, and Heide Davis. *Historic Cemeteries of Portland, Oregon.* Charleston, SC: The History Press, 2021.

Beutler, Mike. Interview by Mark W. Hurlburt. July 1, 2022.

Bishop, Ellen Morris. *In Search of Ancient Oregon: A Geological and Natural History.* Portland, OR: Timber Press, 2003.

Board of County Commissioners Court Order No. 72-302, March 22, 1972.

City of Happy Valley Resolution No. 94-12, September 6, 1994.

Clackamas County Cultural Resource Inventory. Clackamas County Policy and Project Development Division, 1984.

Coats, Sandy. Interview by Mark W. Hurlburt. April 18, 2022.

Cockle, Mrs., and Mrs. Deardorff. "Happy Valley History Tapes." Interview. May 21, 1968.

Confederated Tribes of Grand Ronde. *Chinuk Wawa: As Our Elders Teach Us to Speak It.* Seattle: University of Washington Press, 2012.

County Road 641. Road Book 3. Multnomah County, 1898.

Courtnier, Fran. "The Mount Talbert Cave with Indian Artifacts in Sunnyside, Oregon." Fran Courtnier as related by Allen Hanset, n.d.

Deardorff Cockle, Mabel. "Some Memories of Childhood Days with My Wonderful Grandparents, John and Rachel Deardorff." 1959.

Deardorff Huddle, Olive. "The Old Home Place." 1960.

Eisert, Mrs. Henry. "Happy Valley History." Interview by Mrs. Switzer and Mrs. Wilson. July 16, 1969.

Fegel, Catherine, ed. *The History of Happy Valley, Oregon, 1851–1969*. Portland, OR: Happy Valley School, 1969.

Geppert, August. "Happy Valley History Tapes." Interview. May 14, 1968.

"Getting There." Clackamas County Department of Transportation and Development, 1995.

Grischow, Rolland. "The Sunnyside Community History." Interview by Sandy Van Bemmel. Multnomah Community Television, 1997.

Gustafsson, Erik. Interview by Mark W. Hurlburt. May 13, 2022.

"Happy Valley: A Pathway to the Past: A Driving Tour of the Landmarks of Happy Valley and the Surrounding Area." Happy Valley Elementary School, 1992.

"Happy Valley Comprehensive Plan." City of Happy Valley, May 5, 2009.

"Happy Valley Council Meeting Minutes." November 17, 1965.

Hines, Henry Kimball. *An Illustrated History of the State of Oregon*. Chicago: Lewis Publishing Company, 1893.

Hubbard Cook, Iva. "The Sunnyside Community History." Interview by Sandy Van Bemmel. Multnomah Community Television, 1997.

Hubbard Ulrich, Opal. "The Sunnyside Community History." Interview by Sandy Van Bemmel. Multnomah Community Television, 1997.

Hubbard, Vernon. "The Sunnyside Community History." Interview by Sandy Van Bemmel. Multnomah Community Television, 1997.

Karam, Moses. Interview by Mark W. Hurlburt. August 27, 2022.

Knause, Ed. "Happy Valley History." Interview. July 22, 1969.

Kochendorfer, Lois. "Happy Valley and Zinser Family Memories." Interview by Sandy Van Bemmel. Multnomah Community Television, 1997.

Koper, Steve. Interview by Mark W. Hurlburt. September 8, 2017.

LaPontic, Thelma. "The Sunnyside Community History." Interview by Sandy Van Bemmel. Multnomah Community Television, 1997.

McArthur, Lewis A. *Oregon Geographic Names*. 7th ed., rev. Portland: Oregon Historical Society Press, 2003.

Minutes and records, Sunrise Water Authority, Happy Valley, OR. 2000.

Monner, Mr. "Happy Valley History." Interview. July 16, 1969.

Mount Scott Water District. "Articles of Incorporation." Sunrise Water Authority, Happy Valley, OR. 1930.

Orme, Ron. Interview by Mark W. Hurlburt. June 29, 2020.

Ott, Frank. "History of the Ott Family." 1959.

Ott, Louis. "The Sunnyside Community History." Interview by Sandy Van Bemmel. Multnomah Community Television, 1997.

Ott Piper, Mary. Interview by Mark W. Hurlburt. October 13, 2020.

Pendarvis, Betty. Interview by Mark W. Hurlburt. March 11, 2022.

Peterson, Mrs. Normer. "Happy Valley History." Interview. May 14, 1968.

Portrait and Biographical Record of Portland and Vicinity, Oregon. Chicago: Chapman Publishing Company, 1903.

Rebstock, Karl. Interview by Mark W. Hurlburt. June 6, 2015.

Rebstock, Mrs. Ed. "Happy Valley History." Interview by Mr. Nickory and Mrs. Hicks. July 16, 1969.

Register of County Roads, Road No. 96. Clackamas County, Oregon.

Robnett, James. "Happy Valley Park History." N.d.

"Rock Creek Comprehensive Plan." City of Happy Valley, 2001.

Ruby, Robert H. *A Guide to the Indian Tribes of the Pacific Northwest.* Norman: University of Oklahoma Press, 1992.

Ryckman, Babe. *Grandma, You Were a Daisy!* Self-published, 1993.

Sample, Noreen. "Happy Valley as I Remember It." 1985.

Smith, Barbara. "Park and Field History." 1985.

Strickrott, Archie. "Happy Valley History." Interview by Henry Gilmore. May 7, 1968.

Sunnyside School Centennial: 1884–1885–1984–1985. Sunnyside Elementary School, 1985.

Ulrich Ott, Eva. "The Sunnyside Community History." Interview by Sandy Van Bemmel. Multnomah Community Television, 1997.

"Warranty Deed from J.B. Deardorff and Wife to J. George Zinser." 1890.

"Warranty Deed from J. George Zinser and wife to Charles Rebstock and Bertha Rebstock." 1901.

Witter, Janet. *Place Names in Clackamas County.* Self-published, n.d.

Zinser, Alton. "Happy Valley and Zinser Family Memories." Interview by Sandy Van Bemmel. Multnomah Community Television, 1997.

———. "Zinser Family—As I Know It." 2010.

Zinser, Daryl. "The Sunnyside Community History." Interview by Sandy Van Bemmel. Multnomah Community Television, 1997.

INDEX

Z

ABOUT THE AUTHOR

After graduating with a bachelor of science in history degree from Portland State University, lifelong Happy Valley resident Mark W. Hurlburt has worked in researching, collecting and exhibiting local history. From 2011 to 2015, he worked at the Clackamas County Historical Society's Museum of the Oregon Territory. In 2018, he returned to the museum to volunteer as the librarian in the Wilmer Gardner Research Library. He is also the curator at the Milwaukie Museum, coauthor of *On This Day in Clackamas County* and author of *Images of America: North Clackamas*. He enjoys spending time in the outdoors and with Frankie the wiener dog.